What You W

- That the vast majority of the Internal Revenue (IRC) is not the law itself, but is only evidence-- a representation-- of the actual statutes in force, and like in the game of post-office, the real language has been a bit garbled in transmission.

- That "income", "wages", "self-employment income", "employee", "employer" and "trade or business"-- as these and certain other terms are used within, and in regard to, the tax law-- have narrow legal meanings exclusively involving, and applying to, certain privileged activities, such as holding or administering a government office, or working in one.

- That although the tax statutes make perfectly clear that, for instance, language describing the obligations of "employees"-- and the taxes to which "employees" are subject-- only apply to a small minority of American workers, the distinction is artfully concealed in the IRC representation of the law, and is never forthrightly acknowledged in any IRS publication (although it is obliquely acknowledged whenever necessary for the avoidance of legal jeopardy).

- That an elaborate system has been created which causes some people to whom the tax laws do not otherwise apply (maybe including you) to inadvertently declare themselves to be among the persons to whom those laws *do* apply.

"The revenue laws are a code or system in regulation of tax assessment and collection. They relate to taxpayers, and not to nontaxpayers. The latter are without their scope." United States Court of Claims, Economy Plumbing and Heating v. United States, 470 F.2d 585, at 589 (1972)

Which One Are You?

What Readers Are Saying About 'Cracking the Code':

"...a judicious and thoughtful work written by an American patriot deeply dedicated to the rule of law." "Skepticism and doubt will slowly be replaced with certainty and conviction as Hendrickson systematically walks his readers through the law and the tax code's maze of confusion."
Steve Thomas, The Mackinac Center for Public Policy, Midland, Michigan

"Thank you so much for your exquisitely documented and beautifully written 'Cracking the Code'" "This book is a masterpiece of analysis, clarity and revelation." "This is brain candy for patriots!"
Christiane Sauter, Syracuse, New York

"Wow!!!! I've been studying this for 10 years and haven't gotten anything as clearly as you have put it in your book." "I cannot thank you enough..."
Joyce Cox, Afton, Wyoming

"All American Citizens who truly love their freedom and have a healthy skepticism of the federal government will add this book to their evidentiary foundation..." "...it's a beautiful thing you've done."
John Carpenter, Ann Arbor, Michigan

"Read the book in about 2 days. Very well done. I have been looking at the issue for about 5 years and you distill the info down in a way even the newbies can absorb. Well worth the asking price. I hope this really sells."
Ed Wahler, Fletcher, North Carolina

"EXCELLENT" "...very well written and accurate." "... I would highly recommend."
Dave Wissel, Lebanon, Ohio

"...a valuable tool, and a wealth of knowledge." "Thank you for all your research..."
Arleen Miller, Page, Arizona

"I found the book to be extremely beneficial even though I was fairly knowledgeable on the subject prior to reading the book." "It is definitely on my list of 'recommended reads'. Thanks for a great book."
Phil Patana, St. Louis, Missouri

"...haven't been able to put it down. Great information and fabulously put together!"
Bart Goss, Stockbridge, Georgia

"This is a fabulous book I would highly recommend..."
Larry Golson, Montgomery, Alabama

"...one of the best I have read on the subject and I have been studying the subject for over 30 years."
Bill Richards, Newport News, Virginia

Cracking the Code

The Fascinating Truth About Taxation In America

by

Peter Eric Hendrickson

Also by Peter E. Hendrickson

'Upholding the Law
and Other Observations'

and

'Was Grandpa Really a Moron?
Critical Inquiries for a New American Century'

Printed in the United States of America
First printing July 2003
Second printing April 2004
Third printing December 2004
Fourth Printing March 2005
Fifth Printing July 2005
Sixth Printing December 2005
Seventh Printing September 2006
Eighth Printing May 2007
Ninth Printing February 2008
Tenth Printing September 2008
Eleventh Printing May 2009
Twelfth Printing January 2010
ISBN 0-9743936-0-6

The cover art is a detail from 'Liberty Reclaimed' by the author;
oil on board, 32" x 40"

To order additional copies of this book, or other titles by Peter E. Hendrickson,
visit www.losthorizons.com
or your favorite bookstore

This book is dedicated to my beloved children Kathryn and Thomas, whose rightful legacy it is intended to help preserve, or restore; and to their loving mother-- and my darling wife-- Doreen.

Acknowledgements

Many good Americans recognized the need for critical study of the United States federal tax system over the years before the writing of this book. Several of these folks went to the trouble of making publicly available otherwise difficult-to-acquire documents which I found useful in my own research, and I appreciate their generosity in having done so.

Special thanks go to Randall K. Shelley, who has been a patient sounding board, a muscular devil's advocate and a good friend; and to Sheldon Rose, whose encouragement, wisdom and friendship-- without all of which this book likely would never have been written-- are invaluable to me.

Finally, I would like to thank Charles Adams for the bracing reminder in his charming little book, "Those Dirty Rotten Taxes", that when the French, in their first revolution, threw off the despotic, capitation-fed government to which they had been prey, among the earliest acts of the liberated people was leading virtually every tax collector in the country straight to the guillotine for a *de*-capitation.

Contents

Part Three
(The Nature Of The Crisis)

Appendix

"I don't know what you mean by 'glory'," Alice said.
Humpty Dumpty smiled contemptuously. "Of course you don't-- till I tell you. I meant 'there's a nice knock-down argument for you!'"
"But 'glory' doesn't mean 'a nice knock-down argument'," Alice objected.
"When <u>I</u> use a word," Humpty Dumpty said, in rather a scornful tone, "it means just what I choose it to mean-- neither more nor less."
"The question is," said Alice, "whether you <u>can</u> make words mean so many different things."
"The question is," said Humpty Dumpty, "which is to be master-- that's all."

Foreword

ജ൭ൽ൭ൽ

Let's get this said loud and clear right at the outset: IF YOU HAVE TAXABLE INCOME, YOU ARE SUBJECT TO THE INCOME TAX. Section 1(a) of the Internal Revenue Code says: *"There is hereby imposed on the taxable income of-...* [a tax of varying percentages]*"* Pretty straightforward. Of course, it does raise the question of exactly what is *taxable "income"...*

> *"We must reject... ...the broad contention submitted in behalf of the government that all receipts-- everything that comes in-- are income...".* United States Supreme Court, So. Pacific v. Lowe, 247 U.S. 330, (1918)

"Inclusio unius est exclusio alterius. The inclusion of one is the exclusion of another. The certain designation of one person is an absolute exclusion of all others. ... This doctrine decrees that where law expressly describes [a] particular situation to which it shall apply, an irrefutable inference must be drawn that what is omitted or excluded was intended to be omitted or excluded." Black's Law Dictionary, 6th edition.

*****

It was not until the late 1990's, when the Internal Revenue Code was digitized (and thus made searchable) that it became possible to decipher its deliberately confusing and misleading construction. Only then could complete searches be done of all 3,413,780 or so words (not counting regulations!) for every incidence of "liable", "imposed", "income", "employee", and dozens of other key or misleading terms-- checking every reference, exception, definition and source. Only then could it be established that, as written, the laws behind the code and the taxes that they impose technically comply with the Constitution, just as all the judges have said over the years.

But the same analysis also reveals that, as written, these laws don't apply to most of the receipts of most private citizens. Indeed, the two things are interdependent-- the former couldn't be true unless the latter was also true.

What you will learn as you read this book is that specific Constitutional limitations on the federal government's power to tax *do* shape related law, and have generated a coherent Supreme Court doctrine which clearly and soundly answers the question of what is taxable "income". Both the statutes and the doctrine acknowledge the exemption of the vast majority of private-sector receipts from that taxing power's reach.

However, you will also learn about a complex combination of craft, routine bureaucratic incoherence, and casual-- and not-so-casual-- corruption by virtue of which many people are led to inadvertently allow, and even participate in, the legal transformation of their untaxable earnings *into* taxable "income". Such people are tricked into voluntarily and utterly unnecessarily enabling the diversion of a river of wealth from their own hands, usually never to be seen again.

Thanks to an unhappy coincidence of reiterations and amendments of the law, a series of complicated judicial rulings, and the passage of time and memories, the details of American tax law-- and the principles upon which it is based-- have come to be widely misunderstood. The opportunities presented by that reality have been seized upon, by those paid to maximize revenue flow to the government, to successfully construct an elaborate and deceptive tax scheme rooted in today's Internal Revenue Code.

This scheme capitalizes on widespread public ignorance of general legal doctrine and rules of statutory construction. It practices a careful gauging of extraction levels to the tolerance limits of key demographic segments. It relies upon the concealment of the underlying actual-law-in-force behind the misleading words of the code, which is legally no more than *'evidence of the law'*, and not the law itself.

Fundamental to the scheme is designing that code to be so dauntingly and profoundly confusing as to force the vast majority of those against whom it's directed to abandon even a pretense of personal comprehension. These targets are thus compelled to surrender their decision-making to the code's administrative bureaucracy or a professional class of fixers and go-betweens-- the members of either of which are dependent on the scheme for their own earnings. Unsurprisingly, both assure any who ask that *of course* private-sector receipts are taxed under the law. If pressed, these experts will trot out carefully selected, out-of-context and ambiguous fragments of law calculated to convincingly suggest that what they claim must be in the law, somewhere. But somehow, they never manage to demonstrate exactly where. 'Cracking the Code' is going to provide that missing context, unravel the tangle of deceit and confusion, and make clear that not only is it *not* in there anywhere, what *is* in there is just the opposite.

Plainly stated, the "income" tax scheme is an utterly corrupt and corrosive fraud feeding an ever-more insatiable appetite of a swollen cadre of politically astute private interests and their camp-followers by way of a deliberate campaign of disinformation, intimidation and cunning. It facilitates almost incomprehensible harm to the well-being of all of the rest of us both by the nature and peripheral effects of its implementation, and by the practices and policies which the wealth it transfers make possible.

It is my hope that this book will bring the reader to share that view, and to help in some small way to arm those who'd rather keep, or control the disposition of, their own property with the knowledge by which to do so. It is also my hope that the reader will agree that in this instance, as is the case in so many others, looking after our own interest serves those of society as well. It was not, after all, for idle reasons that the founders imposed strict Constitutional limitations on the taxing power of the federal government. Nor was it merely to protect their own property. Such limitations are essential to meaningful security and the preservation of liberty. As John Adams said, *"The moment the idea is admitted into society that property is not as sacred as the laws of God, and there is not a force of law and public justice to protect it, anarchy and tyranny commence."*

*****

The reader will observe a predisposition of focus throughout this book on receipts from labor, either traded as an "embedded" worker (common-law employee) or as a "free-lance" worker (contractor); as opposed to receipts in the form of interest derived from capital, and the like. This is because such receipts from work represent far-and-away both the biggest pool of wealth and the biggest pool of citizens from which taxes are scammed away.

Some will object to this statistical assertion, having read a hundred times about how the "wealthy"-- read coupon-clipping fat cats-- pay a grossly disproportionate share of the tax burden, and one amounting to the lion's share of the total. These urban legends are reflective of the misunderstandings essential to the success of the tax scheme. While the "wealthy"-- read persons who have produced considerable value for their neighbors, and have been paid a corresponding amount of money-- do indeed pay a disproportionate share (as, if anything, their demand on the public expense is less than that of others), the aggregate percentage of the total tax extraction paid by households with annual receipts over $200,000 is less than one third of the total.

A significant contributor to the erroneous assertions in this regard is a failure to understand that "FICA contributions" are nothing more than "income" taxes indistinguishable both legally and practically from any other, something which will be discussed in greater detail as we proceed. By themselves such "contributions", every penny of which is paid by workers, made up more than 34% of the total federal tax extraction in 2001 (source: OMB).

However, those readers for whom interest, dividends and similar receipts are of paramount concern should note that every principle and point regarding the lawful nature of taxable "income" found herein also apply to that class of receipt-- and will find them, and the information about the structure and nature of the tax laws, illuminating, invigorating and utilitarian. Managers of non-federal corporations and other artificial persons should keep in mind that although the focus of this book is primarily on the application of the "income" tax to natural persons, the meaning of "income" is the same for both kinds of person.

Those who have studied the general subject of taxation in America will note the absence of discussion herein of several revenue acts, as well as various amendments, reforms, and repeals involving the same subject. This book is not intended to be a general exploration of revenue legislation through the years. Rather, it is a study of the lawful scope of any such legislation whenever and however promulgated and the particulars of such legislation as is currently extant to which certain Americans are or can be made subject-- and how these things happen. Enactments which predate the current IRC are selected on the basis of their virtue in clarifying current language therein which is otherwise misleading or unclear. Positive enactments which are incorporated into the IRC are presented in their current form. Emphasis is occasionally added to portions of quotes, cites and excerpts without additional notice.

Clarity obliges the often annoying use of "quotation marks" bracketing certain terms. I don't do this because I like to; it is to distinguish custom-defined legal terms from the common words which they mimic, and for which they might otherwise be mistaken. Such mistakes are a large part of the difficulty many people have in comprehending the truth of the tax scheme, and therefore such clarification is imperative. Please forgive.

Finally, nothing in this book should be construed or relied upon as particular advice or instructions for any particular reader. Each reader must make his or her own independent determination of how the nature, meaning and application of any law affects himself or herself. A searchable current Internal Revenue Code can be found at http://www4.law.cornell.edu/uscode/26/ and the associated regulations can be found at http://www.access.gpo.gov/nara/cfr/cfrhtml_00/Title_26/26tab_00.html. Statutes from the years 1789 - 1875, can be found at http:// memory.loc.gov/ammem/amlaw/lwsl.html; others can be seen at any decent law library. The text of most Supreme and lower court rulings can be found at http://www.findlaw.com

Additional material on the subject of taxes and other matters of law and public policy can be found on my website: http://www.losthorizons.com

Introduction

ꕥ

Until some point within the last year, my faith in the integrity, indeed the lawfulness, of the U.S. Supreme Court was in a sad state of disrepair, and had been for many years. In light of the obvious unconstitutionality of the "income" tax-- as enforced against private citizens within the 50 states-- the failure of the court to declare it so seemed an incontrovertible indictment. At the very least, respect for the rule of law demanded that the apparently incomprehensible statute be ruled void for vagueness, but for all the many years that this tax has been with us, it has been permitted to remain, largely unscathed.

Last year, my faith was restored. Well, that's actually far too strong a statement-- the court still has much to answer for, regarding the "income" tax and a good deal else. But as far as the Constitutionality of that tax as written is concerned, all is well, for the IRC passes Constitutional muster.

*****

How It Happened

Since 1992 when ordered by a rogue and ignorant judge to "comply with all internal revenue laws" (by which was not meant, "Comply with the law", but rather, "Comply with the IRS"; and the circumstances behind which are beyond the scope or purpose of this book-- suffice it to say that they involved a tax protest), I have filed 1040's annually, a practice which had not, previously, been my habit. However, though coerced into producing the form in the typical fashion, I would not allow myself to be compelled to attest to what I knew to be untrue, and so always added to the perjury statement above the signature lines the words, "except insofar as the term "income" is misused herein." This was a reference to the general and explicit presumptive characterization of all wages, salaries, and similar compensations as "income" on the forms and within the instructions. (In 1992 I provided a page length attachment to make this statement, then used the EZ version thereafter). I knew perfectly well that such things, insofar as they have to do with me, cannot be taxable "income", at least not unless I, by endorsing such a characterization (or letting it stand unchallenged) made them so. For 9 years, even after becoming free of this judge's dictates, this was the course of things: I (and eventually my wife Doreen) would fill in the forms, add the disclaimer and send them in, and the IRS would keep a whole lot of money which had been withheld from my earnings during the previous year while paying no attention to my small (but legally significant) protest.

After all, I had just had a taste, actually a pretty big helping, of the disdain which a federal district court judge (and numerous attorneys on both the prosecutorial and defense side of the bar) apparently had for Constitutional limitations on the taxing power, and arguments based upon those limitations were all I was equipped to make. I was familiar with the work of others, such as Lynn Johnston and Irwin Schiff, who had made some limited study of the tax code itself, but even their arguments still ended with the "It doesn't matter what the code says, you can't Constitutionally tax me" conclusion, basically the same approach that I had taken with mine, which had no currency in the courts. (Indeed, until the Cheeks case was ruled on by the Supreme Court in 1991, trial court judges routinely suppressed arguments based upon the Constitutionality of the tax, and even in ruling that Cheek's arguments had to be permitted, the Supreme Court itself declared them to be frivolous). Without such arguments, fighting it out in court seemed doomed, or at least an impossibly long shot.

All of us faced the conundrum that the portions of the code that we had seen were ambiguous at best, and at worst seemed written in defiance of the Constitution; furthermore, who knew what else was to be found within that maze of lawless nonsense that maybe was less ambiguous, and against our position? So, I bided my time, added my disclaimer, wrote my monographs, and continued to study the issue, more-or-less patiently. I intended to resume my more active disagreement with the government on this issue soon enough, but my two children had been born since the start of my last close encounter with a federal court, and I was willing to wait until I was really ready before going back onto the battlefield. But the bad guys wouldn't wait.

In autumn of 2001, for some reason probably born in mindless, banal bureaucratic perversity (though perhaps in recognition of my little disclaimer's nascent legal threat), the agency suddenly informed my wife and me that, because of the disclaimer, it refused to accept our return for 2000. The IRS argued, in essence, that without the endorsement of its characterization of our receipts by an unqualified perjury statement, our return could not be considered as legally filed. Not that it was illegally filed, mind you,... it was treated as not filed at all. They sent us a perjury statement on an otherwise blank piece of paper and indicated that if we would sign it as is and send it back, they would incorporate it into our return and all would be well. If not, we would be considered in default, our deductions and exemptions would not be honored, and interest and penalties would apply and grow.

We had no intention of backing down on this point, and so I began an analysis of the Internal Revenue Code (and other relevant materials) far more intense, and infinitely more productive, than any in which I had ever engaged-- thanks to the marvelous capabilities now afforded to such research by the technology of the information age. This time, I could leapfrog about checking every obscure section reference; search the entire multi-million word document in seconds for every instance of key words and phrases; and draw upon the huge volume of data on the subject posted on the internet by others similarly engaged. This time, I could actually have the grotesque sprawl of incoherence on my screen in my own home. This time, I actually read the damned thing.

The end result of this research was the epiphany regarding the Constitutionality of the code and the behavior of the Supreme Court to which I referred earlier. You will all be happy to learn that the court has been right about the lawfulness of the code, and so have I; Doreen and I have been able to file our last couple of returns with no clarification needed. When you're through with this book, you'll understand how.

*****

'Cracking the Code' is not going to be an easy read. For one thing, there is necessarily a great deal of legal language in the form of statutes and judicial rulings. For another, many readers will find themselves learning that everything they thought they knew about taxation-- and much else about the lawful relationship between citizen and government-- is wrong, which is never easy no matter how it is presented.

However, I trust that the desire to know the truth, not to mention the 30 – 40% of every year's earnings which might be at stake for many readers, will provide sufficient motivation to press on when the going gets difficult; and I assure everyone that even if some portion of this complex material just doesn't seem to make sense initially, by the end of the book you will understand.

The process of overcoming a vast body of multi-dimensional mis-information makes a purely linear exposition of the truth fruitless, if not impossible, and 'Cracking the Code' is organized accordingly. This is not to say that a linear presentation of the taxing statutes cannot be made. The problem is that to understand the statutes, which are written within a framework of constraints typically assumed by the writer to be known by the reader, it is necessary to understand those constraints as well. Some of these constraints are inherent in the principles of jurisdiction; some arise from the rules of statutory construction; others are imposed by the specifications of the Constitution and still more have evolved with Supreme Court jurisprudence. As understanding-- or even just a sense-- of each of these diverse but related elements becomes incorporated into the reader's overall frame of reference, others which had seemed mysterious will become clear. (It is worth noting that the very important benefit of this effect will best be realized if the book is read, as nearly as is possible, without significant interruption.)

So, hang in there, and keep your eyes on the prize. You'll make it, and it's worth it.

Part One

(The Nature Of The Law)

"Come, we shall have some fun now!" thought Alice. "I'm glad they've begun asking riddles-- I believe I can guess that," she added aloud.

"Do you mean that you think you can find out the answer to it?" said the March Hare.

"Exactly so," said Alice.

"Then you should say what you mean," the March Hare went on.

"I do," Alice hastily replied; "at least-- at least I mean what I say-- that's the same thing, you know."

"Not the same thing a bit!" said the Hatter. "Why, you might just as well say that 'I see what I eat' is the same thing as 'I eat what I see'!"

"You might just as well say," added the March Hare, "that 'I like what I get' is the same thing as 'I get what I like'!"

"You might just as well say," added the Dormouse, which seemed to be talking in its sleep, "that 'I breathe when I sleep' is the same thing as 'I sleep when I breathe'!"

About Taxes- Direct v. Indirect

United States Constitution, Article 1, Section 9: *"No capitation, or other direct, Tax shall be laid, unless in Proportion to the Census or Enumeration herein before directed to be taken."*

Before we delve into the history and evolution of the "income" tax, which is the focus of this first part of 'Cracking the Code', it is worthwhile to discuss the general nature of direct taxes and excises. Understanding the principles of the two different classes of taxes, and the jurisdictional issues with which they are connected, is not critical to understanding the tax laws-- the words with which those laws are written clearly express their meanings and limitations. Nonetheless, I believe a comprehension of why those laws are written as they are will be beneficial to the reader. Furthermore, while this book addresses only a few particular areas of the law in detail, the basic principles which will be discussed in this section apply much more broadly, and should serve the interests of the reader accordingly.

*****

All Constitutionally valid federal taxes within the 50 states must be either direct or indirect. Any tax laid on property or people, and thus unavoidable, is a direct tax. Under the Constitution, federal direct taxes which affect citizens of the several states must be apportioned. Apportionment means the division of the total cost of a tax (such as a $10 per house tax X 100 houses = $1000) among the states proportionate to their percentage of the total national population, with the resulting amount being due from the state. The state is free to collect the money however it wishes.

Because of this Constitutional requirement, once someone has come into ownership of money or other property, by fulfilling the terms of a contract, through inheritance, by way of a dividend distribution or however it has been done, that property can only be taxed by means of an apportioned tax. Capitations, or taxes on people, must also be apportioned.

CAPITATION: A poll tax; an imposition which is yearly laid on each person according to his estate and ability.
Bouvier's Law Dictionary, 6th Edition

> *"The taxes which, it is intended, should fall indifferently upon every different species of revenue, are capitation taxes,"... "Capitation taxes, if it is attempted to proportion them to the fortune or revenue of each contributor, become altogether arbitrary. The state of a man's fortune varies from day to day, and without an inquisition more intolerable than any tax, and renewed at least once every year, can only be guessed at."... "Capitation taxes, so far as they are levied upon the lower ranks of people, are direct taxes upon the wages of labour, and are attended with all the inconveniences of such taxes."..." In the capitation which has been levied in France without any interruption since the beginning of the present century, the highest orders of*

people are rated according to their rank by an invariable tariff; the lower orders of people, according to what is supposed to be their fortune, by an assessment which varies from year to year."

This is how Adam Smith, the Father of Economics, defines and describes "capitations" in Book V, CH. II, Art. IV of his seminal treatise on economics and taxation, 'The Wealth of Nations'. This book, published in 1776, instantly rocketed to the heights as the absolute authority on these subjects throughout the Western World. It remains the single most comprehensive resource on the meaning of the Constitutional term "capitation".

Smith deplores capitations as inequitable, inflationary, counterproductive, and destructive of liberty. Importantly, he makes clear that any tax levied upon and/or measured by the exercise of a basic right-- such as the right to life, liberty, the ownership of property, working, or engaging in trade-- is a capitation. Indeed, capitations are alternately known as (and get their name from) "head taxes", because they fall directly upon the head of the citizen. They must be paid by the citizen, and out of his own funds-- simply because he is there, maintaining and exercising his natural powers.

The framers of the Constitution were avid and serious students of Smith's enormously popular work. (During the turmoil of the revolutionary war years alone, Americans bought the equivalent of more than 233,000 copies if proportioned to today's population. This is a solid testament to the esteem in which this substantial and serious work-- 976 pages of densely-packed small type in my copy-- was held.) Agreeing wholeheartedly with his recognition of the evils of unchecked capitations, they specifically prohibited such practices in Article 1 of the Constitution.

Any tax which is not apportioned must be indirect, which is to say, laid upon a wholly optional activity. Indirect taxes, which are denominated as imposts, duties, and excises, are also generally funded by someone other than the remitter (the liable party who sends in the money). Indirect taxes generally take the form of a return to the state of a portion of the benefit conveyed by a special privilege, such as the revenue from trade across the national borders, or the salary or other revenue from a public office. Indirect taxes can also be attendant upon the purchase of a taxed, optional article, by which transaction the vendor becomes liable for a tax paid with the consumer's money. All federal tax within the 50 states must be either direct or indirect-- therefore they must all be either apportioned or optional.

Applying these principles, we can see that while a tax on shopping in general would be a capitation, or direct tax; a tax laid upon some particular thing for which one might or might not shop at one's discretion would be indirect, and thus not a capitation. Similarly, a tax upon being a postal inspector, for instance, to which no one has a right, is an indirect tax; while a tax upon being a graphic artist, to which anyone has a right, would be a capitation. A tax accompanying each transaction involving a taxable article that takes place in your store is an indirect tax, while a tax on having your store open for such transactions-- even if you might be able to recover it from customers on any particular day-- would be a capitation. Black's Law Dictionary, 5th edition, puts it succinctly, defining a "direct tax" as:

> *"One which is demanded from the very persons who it is intended or desired should pay it. Indirect taxes are those which are demanded from one person in the expectation and intention that he should indemnify himself at the expense of another".*

The term "excise" is particularly illustrative of the nature of indirect taxes as specifically on activities. "Excise" means *"a piece of the action".* Excise taxes particularly tax activities associated with the receipt or transfer of property, and the exercise of profitable privilege. In the case of an "income" tax, for instance, it is the activity which produces the property we commonly call 'income' which is being taxed. The income enters into the picture only as a means of measuring the amount (or value) of the taxable activity:

> "*The income tax is, therefore, not a tax on income as such. It is an excise tax with respect to certain activities and privileges which is measured by reference to the income which they produce. The income is not the subject of the tax: it is the basis for determining the amount of tax.*" F. Morse Hubbard, Treasury Department legislative draftsman. House Congressional Record March 27th 1943, page 2580
>
> "*When a court refers to an income tax as being in the nature of an excise, it is merely stating that the tax is not on the property itself, but rather it is a fee for the privilege of receiving gain from the property. The tax is based upon the amount of the gain, not the value of the property.*" John R. Luckey, Legislative Attorney with the Library of Congress, "Frequently Asked Questions Concerning The Federal Income Tax" (C.R.S. Report for Congress 92-303A (1992)).

*****

In addition to prescriptions as to how taxes are laid, there are also jurisdictional issues involved in taxation. A government cannot tax directly or indirectly any thing or any activity outside either its legal or its geographical jurisdiction.

The Constitution establishes a particular geographical area of jurisdiction for the federal government, which includes the District of Columbia, such places as may be formally ceded to that government by the several States for forts, magazines and other needful buildings, and the various territories and possessions:

> *"The Congress shall have Power To exercise exclusive Legislation in all Cases whatsoever, over such District (not exceeding ten Miles square) as may, by Cession of particular States, and the Acceptance of Congress, become the Seat of the Government of the United States, and to exercise like Authority over all Places purchased by the Consent of the Legislature of the State in which the Same shall be, for the Erection of Forts, Magazines, Arsenals, dock-Yards, and other needful Buildings."* U.S. Constitution Article 1, Section 8, Clause 17.

Within this geographical jurisdiction, the United States Congress is permitted to exercise legislative authority of the same general character as that enjoyed by the union States.

All other areas within the union are under the exclusive jurisdiction of one of the several States, and are thus insulated from federal authority except in regard to certain enumerated powers, and federal governmental property and contract rights. As was declared by counsel for the United States before the Supreme Court in United States v. Bevans, 16 U.S. 336 (1818):

> *"The exclusive jurisdiction which the United States have in forts and dock-yards ceded to them, is derived from the express assent of the states by whom the cessions are made. It could be derived in no other manner; because without it, the authority of the state would be supreme and exclusive therein,"*

with the court, in its ruling agreeing:

> *"What, then, is the extent of jurisdiction which a state possesses? We answer, without hesitation, the jurisdiction of a state is co-extensive with its territory;"*

In New Orleans v. United States, 35 U.S. (10 Pet.) 662, 737 (1836), the court reiterates this principle:

> *"Special provision is made in the Constitution for the cession of jurisdiction from the States over places where the federal government shall establish forts or other military works. And it is only in these places, or in the territories of the United States, where it can exercise a general jurisdiction."*

In 1956, the Eisenhower administration commissioned the Interdepartmental Committee for the Study of Jurisdiction Over Federal Areas within the States. The pertinent portion of its report points out that,

> *"It scarcely needs to be said that unless there has been a transfer of jurisdiction (1) pursuant to clause 17 by a Federal acquisition of land with State consent, or (2) by cession from the State to the Federal government, or unless the Federal Government has reserved jurisdiction upon the admission of the State, the Federal Government possess no legislative jurisdiction over any area within a State, such jurisdiction being for exercise entirely by the States, subject to non-interference by the State with Federal functions, and subject to the free exercise by the Federal Government of rights with respect to the use, protection, and disposition of its property".*

*****

Legal (or subject-matter) jurisdiction, simply stated, involves a government's authority over itself and its own creations. A thorough discussion of subject-matter jurisdiction could easily fill a book of its own; it is sufficient for the present to observe that such jurisdiction *does not* involve (or establish) coercive authority to burden-- by taxation or otherwise-- any natural person in the exercise of his or her Rights.

"It could hardly be denied that a tax laid specifically on the exercise of those freedoms would be unconstitutional." United States Supreme Court, Murdock v. Pennsylvania 319 U.S. 105 480-487, (1943)

Because the Rights retained by the people of the several States are many and (mostly) undefined, the practical effect of this limitation is to confine the lawful application of excises to the benefits of privilege granted or facilitated by the government; in other words, the receipt of federal money, or other money gained by virtue of the exercise of federal power.

"The terms "excise tax" and "privilege tax" are synonymous. The two are often used interchangeably." American Airways v. Wallace 57 F.2d 877, 880

"Excises are taxes laid upon the manufacture, sale or consumption of commodities within the country, upon licenses to pursue certain occupations and upon corporate privileges." "...the requirement to pay such taxes involves the exercise of privilege..." U. S. Supreme Court, Flint v. Stone Tracy Co., 220 U.S. 107 (1911).

"A tax upon the privilege of selling property at the exchange... ...differs radically from a tax upon every sale made in any place." "A sale at an exchange differs from a sale made at a man's private office or on his farm, or by a partnership, because, although the subject- matter of the sale may be the same in each case, there are at an exchange certain advantages, in the way of finding a market, obtaining a price, the saving of time, and in the security of payment, and other matters, which are more easily obtained there

than at an office or a farm." U. S. Supreme Court, Nicol v. Ames, 173 U.S. 509 (1899)

"The 'Government' is an abstraction, and its possession of property largely constructive. Actual possession and custody of Government property nearly always are in someone who is not himself the Government but acts in its behalf and for its purposes. He may be an officer, an agent, or a contractor. His personal advantages from the relationship by way of salary, profit, or beneficial personal use of the property may be taxed..." U. S. Supreme Court, United States v. County of Allegheny, 322 US 174 (1944)

The Supreme Court has expressed the character of this limitation several different ways, among them by unambiguously and repeatedly striking down as unconstitutional over the years a number of attempted tax structures the objects of which could not be proven to be related to any delegated power of congress. In its most explicit declaration in this regard, the court says:

"[A]ll that Congress would need to do, hereafter, in seeking to take over to its control any one of the great number of subjects of public interest, jurisdiction of which the states have never parted with, and which are reserved to them by the Tenth Amendment, would be to enact a detailed measure of complete regulation of the subject and enforce it by a so-called tax upon departures from it. To give such magic to the word 'tax' would be to break down all constitutional limitation of the powers of Congress and completely wipe out the sovereignty of the states". Bailey v. Drexel Furniture Co., 259 U.S. 20 (1922)

Such rulings illuminate and enforce the requirement upon Congress to confine its taxing efforts to activities associated with the implementation of its delegated authority, such as the conduct of public offices.

We have the benefit of two recent (though indirect) examples of the effect and meaning of this recognition of the jurisdictional limitations on federal taxes. In the cases of United States v. Lopez 514 U.S. 546 (1995) and Jones v. United States, 99-5739, (2000), the U.S. Supreme Court threw out federal laws restricting the possession of a gun within 1000 feet of a school; and punishing arson; respectively. The court observed that neither act was supported by any credible foundation in any enumerated power of congress within the Constitution. Did Congress come right back and impose a $10,000,000 tax on possession of a gun near a school; or upon the act of pouring and lighting gasoline in a house, which would have effectively accomplished its purposes? It did not, because it cannot.

*****

Focusing the principles of the lawful limitations upon federal taxation on the "income" tax which we are about to particularly explore, we can perceive that unprivileged, outside-of-federal-geographical-jurisdiction work cannot be taxed indirectly by the federal government. As the U.S. Supreme Court says in Butcher's Union Co. v. Crescent City Co., 111 U.S. 746 (1883):

> *"The right to follow any of the common occupations of life is an inalienable right,..."*

and,

> *"It has been well said that 'the property which every man has in his own labor, as it is the original foundation of all other property, so it is the most sacred and inviolable. The patrimony of the poor man lies in the strength and dexterity of his own hands, and to hinder his employing this strength and dexterity in what*

> *manner he thinks proper, without injury to his neighbor, is a plain violation of this most sacred property'."*;

and in Coppage v. Kansas, 236 U.S. 1 (1915):

> *"Included in the right of personal liberty and the right of private property- partaking of the nature of each- is the right to make contracts for the acquisition of property. Chief among such contracts is that of personal employment, by which labor and other services are exchanged for money or other forms of property".*

Other courts have expressed this principle as well:

> *"Since the right to receive income or earnings is a right belonging to every person, this right cannot be taxed as privilege."* Jack Cole Company v. Alfred T. MacFarland, Commissioner, 206 Tenn. 694, 337 S.W.2d 453 Supreme Court of Tennessee (1960)

> *"An income tax is neither a property tax nor a tax on occupations of common right, but is an excise tax...The legislature may declare as 'privileged' and tax as such for state revenue, those pursuits not matters of common right, but it has no power to declare as a 'privilege' and tax for revenue purposes, occupations that are of common right."* Simms v. Ahrens, 271 SW 720 (1925);

The proceeds of such work can only be taxed, of course, with an apportioned direct tax. Widespread (and deliberately?) cultivated misunderstandings to the contrary notwithstanding, no attempt to violate these principles is found within the Internal Revenue Code, as will soon be made clear.

Now, on to the main story...

The Origin Of The "Income" Tax

"It is to be noted that, by the language of the Act, it is not salaries, wages, or compensation for personal services that are to be included in gross income. That which is to be included is gains, profits, and income ***derived from*** *salaries, wages, or compensation for personal services."*

(From the lower court ruling)

Lucas v. Earl, 281 U.S. 111, 50 S. Ct. 241, 74 L. Ed. 731 (1930)

On July 1st, 1862, in the heat of the Civil War and in the face of looming and intractable revenue troubles for the Northern government, its congress passed the Revenue Act of 1862, being,

> *"An Act to provide Internal Revenue to support the Government and to pay interest on the Public Debt".*

Among a lengthy list of measures imposing a variety of excises, duties, license fees and administrative provisions were the following sections:

> *Sec. 86. And be it further enacted, That on and after the first day of August, eighteen hundred and sixty-two, there shall be levied, collected, and paid on all salaries*

of officers, or payments to persons in the civil, military, naval, or other employment or service of the United States, including senators and representatives and delegates in Congress, when exceeding the rate of six hundred dollars per annum, a duty of three per centum on the excess above the said six hundred dollars; and it shall be the duty of all paymasters, and all disbursing officers, under the government of the United States, or in the employ thereof, when making any payments to officers and persons as aforesaid, or upon settling and adjusting the accounts of such officers and persons, to deduct and withhold the aforesaid duty of three per centum, and shall, at the same time, make a certificate stating the name of the officer or person from whom such deduction was made, and the amount thereof, which shall be transmitted to the office of the Commissioner of Internal Revenue, and entered as part of the internal duties;...

Sec. 90. And be it further enacted, That there shall be levied, collected, and paid annually, upon the annual gains, profits, or income of every person residing in the United States, whether derived from any kind of property, rents, interest, dividends, salaries, or from any profession, trade, employment, or vocation carried on in the United States or elsewhere, or from any other source whatever, except as hereinafter mentioned, if such annual gains, profits, or income exceed the sum of six hundred dollars, and do not exceed the sum of ten thousand dollars, a duty of three per centum on the amount of such annual gains, profits, or income over and above the said sum of six hundred dollars; if said income exceeds the sum of ten thousand dollars, a duty of five per centum upon the amount thereof exceeding six hundred dollars;..." (The section goes on to extend the tax to citizens residing abroad who are not government workers at a rate of 5% and without the $600 exemption).

Sec. 93. And be it further enacted,...that any party, in his or her own behalf,...shall be permitted to declare, under oath or affirmation, the form and manner of which shall be prescribed by the Commissioner of Internal Revenue, that he or she was not possessed of an income of six hundred dollars, liable to be assessed according to the provisions of this act, or... has been assessed elsewhere... and shall thereupon be exempt from an income duty; or, if the list or return of any party shall have been increased...,... he or she may be permitted to declare,... the amount of his or her annual income,... liable to be assessed,... and the same so declared shall be received as the sum upon which duties are to be assessed and collected.

So, in 1862, in the first artless and innocent iteration of an American "income" tax, an excise with provisions for withholding is laid upon the pay of government workers. At the same time, the excise is separately laid upon *"gains, profits, or income"* that might be *derived from* the pay (or other sources) of private-sector persons and government workers alike (such as through investments in taxable entities).

By its explicit, separate, and otherwise unnecessary identification in section 86 of the remuneration (pay) of government workers as taxable-- and taxed-- this original enactment provides a rare, forthright statutory acknowledgement that the remuneration of private-sectors workers is not. After all, if *"gains, profits, or income derived from"* pay is the same thing as the pay itself, the pay of government workers identified in section 86 would be being taxed under section 90, and the relevant portion of section 86 would be nonsensically superfluous. This clearly lawful distinction will not, and could not, change through the many less candid re-enactments and modifications of the tax since. The similar exclusion of private-sector receipts of any *other* kind from the legal category of 'taxable' is not, unfortunately, as lucidly spelled out in this act other than in their sharing the implications of the qualifier *"derived from"*, but is satisfactorily clarified elsewhere, as we shall see.

Subsequent acts changed the rate, and eventually added progressivity, but the imposition of the tax, and the specifications of-- and exclusions from-- its object remain. (There is a persistent factoid of misinformation to the effect that this 1862 act was repealed in 1872. While it is true that a few portions of the earlier act were repealed or modified in the revenue act of December 24th, 1872, sections 86, 90, and 93, reproduced above, were not among them. Enforcement of the "income" duty *was* allowed to temporarily lapse at that time, but it was never repealed.)

In 1880, the act was tested in the Supreme Court by an attorney named Springer, who asserted that it amounted to an unapportioned (and therefore unconstitutional) direct tax when applied to his professional earnings (all of which he allowed to be characterized as "income" for purposes of the challenge, despite apparently having a mix of both federally-connected and non-federally-connected earnings), and to interest on bonds that he held (Springer v. United States, 102 U.S. 586 (1880)). The court unremarkably ruled against Springer, in a brief opinion of interest only due to its observation that to treat a tax on "incomes" as direct-- and therefore apportioned-- would be inequitable because,

> *"Where the population* [of a state] *is large and the incomes are few and small, it would be intolerably oppressive".*

If "income" is understood as meaning 'pay', or 'all that comes in', the court's observation is gibberish. It's possible that one of the welfare states of today might come to have a large population with few people making a living, but in 1880 there certainly was no such place. With its observation, the court was matter-of-factly confirming the distinction between "incomes" and the common receipts of private-sector persons, just as had the 1862 act.

*****

In 1894, Congress re-enacted the "income" tax-- combining certain elements of the original sections 86 and 90 to explicitly require the inclusion of "*the salary or other compensation paid to any person in the employment or service of the United States... in the calculation of* [taxable] *total gains, profits or income*" of that person; and again providing for withholding. The new act was promptly challenged in the Supreme Court, insofar as it attempted to characterize dividends paid by an investment fund as taxable "gains, profit, or income". Ruling on the question in Pollock v. Farmers Loan & Trust, 157 U.S. 429 and 158 U.S. 601 (1895), the court made two important declarations prior to its final ruling, the first being,

> *"The power to tax real and personal property and the income from both, there being an apportionment, is conceded: that such a tax is a direct tax in the meaning of the Constitution has not been, and, in our judgment, cannot be successfully denied: ...".*

The court is saying that a tax connected with receipts from property already acquired was indistinguishable in essence from a tax upon the property itself-- without regard to any exercise of privilege in deriving such receipts-- because the mere possession of the property is meaningless without deriving gain from it. In other words, even otherwise taxable "income" is untaxable if connected with personally owned property. The court referred to Springer, indicating regret that the earlier ruling had not distinguished between the plaintiff's two types of receipts because while those reflecting profitable activity from his profession might have been properly subject to an excise, those from his bonds should not have been.

The second important observational element of the Pollock ruling, arrived at after an exhaustive recital of the history of taxation in Great Britain and the United States, was that,

> *"Ordinarily, all taxes paid primarily by persons who can shift the burden upon some one else, or who are under no legal compulsion to pay them, are considered indirect* [excise] *taxes;"*

and that (as subsequently summarized in a later ruling),

> *"...taxation on income was in its nature an excise entitled to be enforced as such,"*

-- in other words, indirectly, upon an optional exercise of privilege.

The Supreme Court And The Meaning Of "Income"

The Supreme Court, in the Pollock decision, DID NOT rule the "income" tax unconstitutional. It merely ruled that the measurement of the tax by receipts derived from the use of personal property is unconstitutional, because the property itself is untaxable:

> *"The tax imposed by sections 27 to 37, inclusive, of the act of 1894, so far as it falls on the income of real estate, and of personal property, being a direct tax, within the meaning of the constitution, and therefore unconstitutional and void, because not apportioned according to representation, all those sections, constituting one entire scheme of taxation, are necessarily invalid."*

Like all of the "income" tax acts over the years, the act of 1894 had coyly declined to spell out what qualifies as "income", other than the compensation of federal workers. It instructed government offices and agencies to treat and report their payments as such, by means which we will examine later, but left to all others the task of recognizing when the law does and does not apply to them. In Pollock's case, the railroad-owning Farmer's Loan and Trust Company (now Citibank of New York) had indicated its intention to declare its profits as "income" and pay taxes on them before distributing what was left to Pollock and other investors as dividends. His suit established only that such dividends and their like could not be treated as "income" even if associated with a taxable activity. Nonetheless, the case was enormously significant. In large part, the 1894 act had had its sights set on the huge profits being made by investments in ventures such as railroads, declared by the Supreme Court during the 1880's to amount to federal instrumentalities. The ruling thus took the meat-and-potatoes of the "income" tax's potential to the federal treasury off the table-- there wasn't much left by which the tax on federal salary "income" could be supplemented.

In response to the Pollock ruling, the Sixteenth Amendment-- *"The Congress shall have power to lay and collect taxes on incomes, from whatever source derived, without apportionment among the several states, and without regard to any census or enumeration."*-- was declared ratified in 1913, promptly followed in October of the same year by a new revenue act.

Almost immediately, the Supreme Court had occasion to address the new amendment, in Brushaber v. Union Pacific R. Co., 240 U.S. 1 (1916). The plaintiff in the case, Frank Brushaber, sought to defeat the taxation of dividends from *his* railroad investments under the new act. He cleverly suggested that the definition of "income" to which it and the amendment referred should be understood as having been expanded so as to encompass the objects of a capitation or other direct tax, yet without apportionment. His notion was to exploit the various Constitutional problems which would naturally arise from such a misunderstanding. The court patiently corrected his error, declaring that the amendment had done nothing more than establish that the excise on "income" can be laid without regard to its connection with personal property. The court also repeats and reinforces its declaration from the Pollock ruling that such a tax can only be laid as an excise-- noting that the Article 1, Section 9 Constitutional prohibition on unapportioned direct taxes had not been repealed.

> *"We are of opinion, however, that the confusion is not inherent, but rather arises from the conclusion that the 16th Amendment provides for a hitherto unknown power of taxation; that is, a power to levy an income tax which, although direct, should not be subject to the regulation of apportionment applicable to all other direct taxes. And the far-reaching effect of this erroneous assumption will be made clear by generalizing the many contentions advanced in argument to support it..."*
>
> ...
>
> *"But it clearly results that the proposition and the contentions under it, if acceded to, would cause one provision of the Constitution to destroy another; that is, they would result in bringing the provisions of the Amendment exempting a direct tax from apportionment into irreconcilable conflict with the general requirement that all direct taxes be apportioned."*

The court is pointing out that the amendment had in no way modified or expanded the meaning of the word "income" as lawfully used in a taxing statute. Nor had it changed the requirement that the application of any such statute must be confined to the forms and proper subjects of an excise-- that is, the exercise of privilege. The amendment simply provides that the constitutionality of such a tax can no longer be challenged by reference to the property connected with any particular "income". Such a challenge, in other words, can only argue against the taxability of the activity to which the "income" tax is being applied. The court upholds the 1913 revenue act at issue in Brushaber as being consistent with these requirements. All that it seeks to tax are *"gains, profits, or income from whatever source derived"* just as had the act of 1862, with no language seeking to tax common, private-sector receipts, such as unprivileged pay-for-work.

(Nonetheless, language excluding "income exempt from taxation by the fundamental law [the Constitution]" is consistently deployed in one way or another in connection with "income" tax enactments from this point forward.

The earliest deployment of this language-- which is in any event probably included as a pre-emptive defense against the law being struck down for overreach-- may have been intended to distinguish those receipts not subject to the tax under any circumstances from those which are, per the provisions of Article 1, Section 9 of the U.S. Constitution. Arguably, in 1913, the fact that within the context of the tax "income" had acquired a fixed meaning exclusively confined to the latter of these categories (something explicitly observed by the Supreme Court 7 years later-- see 'The Plot Thickens' for more on this) was a nuance unrecognized by the Congressional legislative draftsmen.

However, it is at least equally likely that this language was and is intended to protect the tax from challenges based on its application to certain forms of "income" technically subject to the tax but which is also subject to special rules under the Constitution, such as the compensation paid to the President and federal judges, which is to remain undiminished during the office-holder's tenure. The question of how these provisions could be reconciled with the tax led to much debate and litigation during the first third of the 20th century.)

The Brushaber court also seizes the opportunity to reaffirm the core element of the "income" tax by pointing out that the *only* way to square the Sixteenth Amendment with Article 1, Sections 2 and 9 of the Constitution was through a fixed, customized definition of what had been a legal term and was now a Constitutional term: "income". Because a tax on "income" is *necessarily* an excise, whatever is thus taxed as "income" MUST be confined to such things to which an excise can properly be applied. As the court puts it, taxation on "income" is,

> "... *in its nature an excise entitled to be enforced as such unless and until it was concluded that to enforce it would amount to accomplishing the result which the requirement as to apportionment of direct taxation was adopted to prevent, in which case the duty would arise to disregard form and consider substance alone, and hence subject the tax to the regulation as to apportionment which otherwise as an excise would not apply to it"*

In other words, if the tax should mutate or be construed so as to embrace objects not appropriate for an excise, such as "all that comes in", for instance (therefore becoming, de facto, a capitation, or other direct tax), it would have to be implemented under the rule of apportionment regardless of the fact that it was still being called only an "income" tax.

In the same year as the Brushaber decision, the court acknowledges the concurrent jurisdictional limitation of the taxing power of Congress in Stanton v. Baltic Mining Co, 240 U.S. 103 (1916):

> *"Mark, of course, in saying this we are not here considering a tax... entirely beyond the scope of the taxing power of Congress, and where consequently no authority to impose a burden, either direct or indirect, exists. In other words, we are here dealing solely with the restriction imposed by the 16th Amendment on the right to resort to the source whence an income is derived in a case where there is power to tax"*

Two years later, in Peck v. Lowe, 247 U.S. 165 (1918), the court observed again that the 16th Amendment in no way expanded that jurisdictional reach, saying:

> *"The Sixteenth Amendment, although referred to in argument, has no real bearing and may be put out of view. As pointed out in recent decisions, it does not extend the taxing power to new or excepted subjects, but merely removes all occasion, which otherwise might exist, for an apportionment among the states of taxes laid on income, whether it be derived from one source or another."*

Here are a few other relevant citations accenting, with varying acuity, some of the Brushaber court's points:

> *"The Treasury cannot by interpretive regulations, make income of that which is not income within the meaning of the revenue acts of Congress, nor can Congress, without apportionment, tax as income that which is not income within the meaning of the 16th Amendment."* Helvering v Edison Bros. Stores, 133 F2d 575. (1943)

> *"The provisions of the Sixteenth Amendment conferred no new power of taxation but simply prohibited the complete and plenary power of income taxation possessed by Congress from the beginning from being taken out of the category of indirect taxation to which it inherently belonged . . ."* Stanton v. Baltic Mining Co., 240 U.S. 103 (1916)

> *"Constitutionally the only thing that can be taxed by Congress is "income." And the tax actually imposed by Congress has been on net income as distinct from gross income. The tax is not, never has been, and could not*

constitutionally be upon "gross receipts"... " Anderson Oldsmobile, Inc. vs Hofferbert, 102 F Supp 902 (1952)

"The general term "income" is not defined in the Internal Revenue Code" US v Ballard, 535 F2d 400, 404 (1976)

*****

As its jurisprudence expressing and implementing the Brushaber principle matured, the Supreme Court devoted a fair amount of attention to the phrase, "gains, profits and income", in an effort to further clarify the necessary elements of what could be taxed as "income". In its ruling in So. Pacific v. Lowe, 247 U.S. 330, (1918), for instance, the high court affirms the declaration by the court below that,

> *"... 'income', as used in the statute should be given a meaning so as [not] to include everything that comes in. The true function of the words 'gains' and 'profits' is to limit the meaning of the word 'income'."*

Although the issue central to this case involves the application of the law to dividends paid by a railroad-owning corporation, and the 'profit' aspect is not critical to our present analysis of the law as written since no tax has been imposed on private-sector receipts, profitable or otherwise, it is worth our while to indulge a brief diversion into its implications. The revenue acts, after all, draw, and can draw, no distinction whatever between the meaning of "income" to a corporation and the meaning of "income" to a natural person:

> *"It is obvious that these decisions in principle rule the case at bar if the word "income" has the same meaning in the Income Tax Act of 1913 that it had in the Corporation Excise Tax Act of 1909, and that it has the same scope of meaning was in effect decided in Southern Pacific Co. v. Lowe 247 U.S. 330, 335, where it was assumed for the purposes of decision that there*

> *was no difference in its meaning as used in the act of 1909 and in the Income Tax Act of 1913. There can be no doubt that the word must be given the same meaning and content in the Income Tax Acts of 1916 and 1917 that it had in the act of 1913. When to this we add that in Eisner v. Macomber, supra, a case arising under the same Income Tax Act of 1916 which is here involved, the definition of "income" which was applied was adopted from Strattons' Independence v. Howbert, arising under the Corporation Excise Tax Act of 1909, with the addition that it should include "profit gained through sale or conversion of capital assets," there would seem to be no room to doubt that the word must be given the same meaning in all the Income Tax Acts of Congress that was given to it in the Corporation Excise Tax Act, and that what that meaning is has now become definitely settled by decisions of this Court."*
> Merchants' Loan & Trust Co. v. Smietanka 255 U.S. 509 (1921),

...and it is important for an overall understanding of lawful taxation to recognize that "income" which can be lawfully taxed must not only be a consequence of the exercise of a privilege, but it must also involve a meaningful gain. Even government workers otherwise properly taxed on receipts associated with their conduct of a public office can't be taxed on money received as reimbursements, for instance. The key virtue of this exercise will be in illuminating why, among other reasons, under this particular settled doctrine of the court private-sector proceeds of work (in particular) cannot be taxed under an "income" tax.

*****

Let's begin with a simple mental exercise: Suppose that you were a shepherd who needed a new pair of shoes. You take a sheep down to your neighbor the cobbler, who trades you a pair of shoes for your sheep. You're both happy, you with the shoes that you didn't have before, and your neighbor with a week or two's worth of dinner. Did either of you receive "income" (defined, for the purpose of this exercise, solely as profit)? Clearly not. The market value of your sheep was equaled by the market value of the shoes, and neither you nor the cobbler made a profit. Now, let's suppose that, rather than carrying your sheep to the cobbler's, you gave him an IOU which can be redeemed for one sheep (or traded to someone else for one sheep's worth of value in other goods, who will trade for it knowing that they can redeem it for a sheep, or trade it away themselves). Now you've got the shoes and the cobbler has a claim on a sheep or its equivalent value. Any profits ("income") now? Of course not.

OK, how about this-- instead of an IOU for one of your sheep, you give the cobbler the note you're holding from your other neighbor, the carpenter, for a day's worth of carpentry, (or its equivalent, as explained earlier), that you got last week in trade for one of your sheep. Any profit or "income" now? Still no. And how about that carpenter, who redeems his note by doing a day's worth of work for the cobbler. When the cobbler gives him the note, debt paid, has the carpenter received "income"? Clearly not.

No one received any "income" in our example because by merely trading what they already possessed for it's equivalent value in someone else's property, none of our citizens increased their wealth, they simply converted pre-existing assets to a different form. Some would make the argument that our carpenter is an exception, saying that he didn't really trade anything, he simply was paid for his time-- getting something for nothing. That argument implies that an individual doesn't own, as a resource, his or her time/labor, leaving one to wonder to whom they would propose that it *does* belong; it also presumes or implies that the time/labor available to the carpenter, as to all of us, is not an all too finite resource--an absurdity not worthy of rebuttal. I will dismiss such arguments with the observations that the consumer of the carpenter's work did not acquire its benefits by magic; and the carpenter could have spent his days making shoes like the cobbler or raising sheep like the shepherd if he wished, or studying to improve his skills. There is no practical difference between any of these choices, they are all just ways of using ones time/labor, and the specialization in one or the other toward which individuals naturally gravitate as they discover where their talents and interests lie simply maximizes the benefit to the whole community. Besides, the very fact that someone would offer value in exchange for the carpenter's time/labor establishes it as a legitimate tradable good.

*****

Douglas Adams, in 'Life, the Universe and Everything' one of the books in his wonderful 'Hitchhiker's Guide to the Galaxy' series, describes a society that elected to make leaves legal tender, imagining that with this choice they would immediately all be rich, and without any effort! Eventually, they are forced to burn down all the trees, in order to curb inflation...

It is vitally important for the sake of clear thinking to understand that ***all*** tradable goods of any kind, including sheep and shoes as well as work (and by extension the notes or tokens, sometimes called money, used to facilitate the trading process), represent a unit of time/labor. If goods could be acquired without an expenditure of time/labor, they would have no value. They might still be desirable, as air is desirable, even necessary, but of no tradable value due to being attainable without any effort. For instance if gold, a tradable good long used as a form of money, were as common as sand and as easily acquired, we might still like to wear it as jewelry but we would not use it as money, for it would not represent any meaningful unit of time/labor. It can be used as money only because acquiring it requires effort in the mining process, both in locating and extracting it, rendering it a tradable good with an inherent value. The same is true of our shepherd's sheep. If a sheep could be had by anybody, anytime, by simply stepping outside and grabbing one-- without hunting for it or husbanding it-- sheep would have no value, and neither the cobbler nor the carpenter would offer their goods in trade for one. The value in these goods comes from the time/labor expenditure necessary to acquire them. All tradable goods consist of time/labor, either converted to a hard product through the picking of the apples, the raising of the sheep, the making of the shoes, etc.; rendered in its original form as service (which is to say, doing the same things for someone else); or as a combination of the two.

As an example of that last form, which is the most common form of tradable good in our complex economy, let us examine the shoemaker, who trades 'x' for his materials, and then sells (trades) his shoes for 'x + y'?! Surely he has made a profit, and acquired "income"?!

What the shoemaker has done is mixed his time/labor, which is one of his resources, with his raw materials-- creating more value for the raw materials as they become refined into a product of a different kind, but only to the same degree as the cobbler's expenditure of his time and energy. If the cobbler attempted to sell his shoes for more than the value of the resources consumed in the production process, his customers, who also can acquire leather and thread, and also have time and energy, could make them for themselves. If those customers were to make that choice, and fashion their own shoes, they could surely not be charged with having received "income", represented by some calculation of the increased value of the leather and thread! No more can the cobbler.

This is not to say that the cobbler does not enjoy a competitive advantage in evaluating his goods for the market; he can take advantage of his greater experience and superior efficiency in making his products, making his expenditure relatively less than that faced by his customers in contemplating whether to buy or make their own. But that same advantage is enjoyed by all specialists in the market, and thus does not change the dynamic of trading value for equal value, with gain to none, and in any case does not represent some magical infusion of resource or value not originating from (and belonging to), the cobbler. (That any producer may also bring special artistry to his or her work, adding value beyond that of the other resources consumed, is true as well, but does not conflict with the basic point).

Theoretically, we all could make our own consumable products-- spending our time hunting for materials and sitting around fashioning the things we need. We would simply lose the greater efficiency of specialization which provides for less cost of time/labor in production. Choosing the advantages of specialization, and the necessary mechanism of trade to actualize its benefits, does not add to our inherent personal resources despite allowing us to acquire more and better goods than we could make or acquire were we to live as hermits.

All of our players in this example are participants in a specialization-based market economy. It is, in every detail, the same market economy in which you and I participate, just rendered a little tricky to perceive by the use of different terms for key ingredients-- most notably IOUs (or notes) for money, and the references to work as a tradable good. The money that we use today in the United States is simply IOUs which, for convenience and efficiency, we have recently (about a hundred years ago) decided should be written by a central authority for the sake of uniformity. After all, goes the argument, transactions are often wide-ranging in the players they involve and the distances and layers of ownership and obligation that they navigate. That centralization removes from money the personal IOU obligation of the original notes. Thus a dollar bill, for example, no longer has the name of the carpenter on it, identifying him as the origin of the note and his time/labor as the backing for the note's value, because the market's participants all understand that everyone's notes are tradable for everyone's goods, since everyone's tradable goods ultimately are of the same nature.

It was only in the early 20th century that the American economy began this experiment with centralized printing of money; prior to that time paper money consisted exclusively of banknotes issued by individual financial institutions redeemable upon demand by the bank for a tradable good such as gold or silver, as well as drafts against personal accounts. Our Federal Reserve scrip of today will not be redeemed by the issuing institution, but is imbued with value by our general agreement as participants in the market to accept it as a trading medium. This distinction does not mitigate its nature as a token symbolizing time/labor. When you are paid dollars by one participating member of the market, you are receiving notes of obligation against the common pool of market wealth equal to your contribution to that pool, and redeemable in the form of any other equally valued portion of the pool. That pool is the aggregate of all the time/labor invested by the participants in that market.

The true nature of money is an important issue for society for many reasons, but for our purposes here, it is because those benefiting from already confusing "income" tax laws try to further muddy the waters by focusing our attention on the acquisition of money-- as though the tax were laid upon money, rather than on taxable (privileged) activities, the extent of which is measured by the money they produce. Such beneficiaries like very much to have the legal object of the "income" tax be a blurry moving target in the minds of their victims, and they are delighted to borrow from the widespread confusion regarding the nature of money.

Money, of course, being property, can only be taxed by a direct (therefore, apportioned) tax. Furthermore, it is important to keep in mind that the money itself, particularly our printed scrip form, has no inherent value at all-- its sole value is in its representation of, or ability to command redemption by, labor. You can't eat the money, you can only eat the product of labor for which the money can be traded. When you give someone money, you're actually giving them, at bottom, labor; when you receive money, you are receiving debt instruments representing labor owed to you. In a complex economy, the distance between currency and the foundational labor of acquiring, defending, coaxing yield-- and eventually surplus-- from the land; and the basic production of all the other things made possible by that fundamental formation of wealth is great indeed, but that labor remains the source of value of every dollar.

To summarize all of this in a nutshell: remuneration for work literally IS labor; and the seizure (whether called a tax or anything else) of remuneration that is the result of simply working for a living amounts to slavery. There is no meaningful distinction that can be drawn between the taking of 25% of a worker's pay in taxes with which to purchase [his or his competitor's] products and services, and forcing that worker into a government factory to produce those products and services for free 2 hours out of every 8-hour workday. That the latter would be grossly unconstitutional needs hardly be said; that the former also is should be clear as well. In light of the requirement that a lawfully taxable activity be measured by *profit* (without even concerning ourselves with the *privilege* requirement), it is equally clear that in neither case can "income" be alleged. Just as it is impossible to characterize two hours of labor in the government factory as profit, the two hours worth of work taken as money also fails the test.

(For someone working for the taxing authority, of course, the "tax" would be nothing but a pay cut, and would represent a voluntarily accepted condition of "employment", all remuneration from which constitutes, by law, profit).

*****

This discussion of labor and money allows an only *slightly* tortured segue to another topic by virtue of the underlying wisdom awaiting discovery, as so often is the case, behind words long associated with those two subjects. In this case, it is our expression "making money" that reveals the truth about money's nature; for restated with more accuracy and clarity, what we mean by these words is "creating wealth", a true description of our behavior when we expend our labor-- wealth being nothing more than the durable product of labor, whether that labor is devoted directly to physical production or improvement, or is in the form of services by which others are made able to so directly produce. The creation, of course, is the property of the creator; by which principle both our own wealth is secured to us, and that created by virtue of government privilege is made amenable to a government claim of an ownership interest.

This same principle informs the nature of lawful government and its proper authority, and the laws that can be made under that authority; which we will briefly explore next. While a thoughtful and informed perspective on those subjects is not absolutely necessary to understand and apply the tax law as written, it is nonetheless very helpful in that endeavor-- and a virtue in any free and sovereign citizen.

Regarding The Law And Its Virtues

A society transforms itself into a state through the adoption of law. By the use of law, what had been more-or-less spontaneous interactions of conflict are regularized and formalized. This more reliably secures to each participant the benefits of predictability and stability (and that of a superior defensive capacity against individuals or organizations which might seek to subjugate them). Law provides these benefits by replacing the vagaries of custom and tradition with demonstrably authorized, written, unambiguous and procedurally scrupulous rules governing the interactions of the participants, backed by the cooperative and coordinated actions of each such participant.

When performing its legitimate purpose, the law is a great blessing to all. When carelessness or ignorance permit its application to illegitimate purposes, the enormous power of a coordinated and cooperative society becomes a potent tool for the satisfaction of private interests and the abuse of political targets, as well as the imposition of tyranny. It is possible to measure the character of that which claims status as law by its conformity to three essential principles: 1. Legitimacy of authority; 2. Clarity of command; and 3. Conformity with established procedures of notice.

Though once the very pinnacle of respect for legitimate rule of law (and the most richly rewarded beneficiary thereof), the United States has fallen deeply from that high ground. An analysis of the essential principles of law will reveal how we have stumbled, and provide guidance as to how to once again find the right path.

But first, Sovereignty

Before discussing the characteristics of law, which is the product of a state, it is necessary to briefly comment on sovereigns, who are the precursors to the state. A sovereign is a free-standing, independent agent, whose right to exist and act are inherent by nature. While much weird and degenerate philosophy has been fabricated over the centuries alleging social contracts, mystical fatherlands, divine right and the like, ad nauseum, the simple and incontrovertible facts are:

- *No human being can assert a claim of authority by right over any other human being;*
- *All human agencies are merely subordinate constructs which can claim no authority beyond that of their creators; furthermore, such agencies can assert nothing for themselves, and assertions made on their behalf can have no demonstrable standing beyond that of the speaker or speakers-- who are just other human beings;*
- *No one can claim rights superior in quantity or quality to those of anyone else.*

Therefore, regardless of whether or not each of us really has a right to act freely, no one else has a right to interfere with our acting freely. So, we are all sovereign by default at least, if not by design. Our power-to-act is not dependent upon or answerable to any other person or any other person's creation.

States, on the other hand, are not sovereign, except as to other states. This will be discussed in more detail below.
On to the law...

*****

1. Legitimacy of Authority

The starting point of any law is the authority of the legislators. A law can only issue from an agency to which those upon whom the law will act have delegated appropriate authority. Such authority can be broad or narrow, depending upon the wishes of the delegator, but is in all cases limited and explicit-- for the authority to withdraw, modify or define any delegation cannot itself be delegated. A delegation, after all, is an assignment, not a negotiation; furthermore, only that over which an individual has authority himself can be delegated to another.

"Authority" means *creatorship*, or, because the attributes of the created are as designed by the creator, *the rule of the created by the creator. (The root of the word is the Latin, "auctor", which means "creator". The principle which is addressed here doesn't rest on semantics, of course, but as is often the case, the etymology of the appropriate term can clear away cobwebs of confusion spun by its promiscuous misuse.)* Being possessed of authority over their own decisions, individuals can delegate the making of such decisions to an agent, and can agree to adopt such decisions as their own and act accordingly. The quality of self-directed independence (sovereignty) however, is not under human authority and therefore cannot be delegated to the state. Thus, the state can have no standing or interest on behalf of which its spokesmen may properly dispute, redefine, qualify or interpret the terms of the delegation. The state is not a party to the deal and is, insofar as its own nature is concerned, voiceless.

It is, after all, the delegation itself which creates the state. The creation cannot partake of the decision by which it is created; that is, the state cannot authorize its own authority. Not only is such a lifting-oneself-up-by-one's-own-bootstraps impossible temporally, it is also impossible legally, for it would create a dysfunctional and irresolvable tension between competing authorities. The creation would argue with the creator, from equal standing, as to what authority has been granted it-- the legal equivalent of two bodies occupying the same space at the same time.

Further, even if the metaphysical impediments could be overcome, such a delegation *could not* be accomplished, for it would constitute an unmistakable act against the delegator's own interests, be evidence of an unsoundness of mind, and therefore be void. Basic logic and legal principle establish that one cannot competently or effectively choose to divest oneself of the power to delegate, or to be the sole determinant of the meaning and extent of delegations made, or otherwise compromise one's sovereignty. Simple natural law precludes the possibility as well-- as Samuel Adams, the Father of the American Revolution, points out,

> *"If men, through fear, fraud, or mistake, should in terms renounce or give up any natural right, the eternal law of reason and the grand end of society would absolutely vacate such renunciation. The right to freedom being the gift of Almighty God, it is not in the power of man to alienate this gift and voluntarily become a slave."*

Nor, of course, can one individual be bound by delegative choices made by another. Any individual has only the capacity to delegate his own deliberative and decision-making powers, not those of his neighbor.

Although these points about the subordinate, voiceless nature of the state seem elementary upon examination, violations of the principle are now routine in America, in service to factions wishing to exercise illegitimate power for their own benefit at the expense of their neighbors. This is done through a corrupt and corrupting sophistry which twists legitimacy of authority and sovereignty into conveniences of the politically powerful.

The process can be perceived by consideration of any victimless "crime". Because the relevant behavior involves no conflict in regard to which the participants might have an interest in the benefits of law, no credible or proper basis for a relevant delegation authorizing state involvement can be alleged. Also, of course, no victim with standing from which to seek suppressive redress can be called upon. Factions which wish to nonetheless assert power over their neighbors in regard to the disapproved behavior must overcome these infirmities.

To do so, they posit a mysticism by which the aggregate mass of delegators, personified by the state, has, *prest-o change-o!*, acquired sovereignty-- and sovereignty of superior stature to that of any of its individual parts. This magical sovereign claims standing as an aggrieved party where no real one can make a complaint, so as to legitimize calling upon itself for remediation from the "offense". Godlike, this sovereign exists at all times and in all places, available to be offended against whenever and wherever any vile perpetrator acts, and, being relieved of the necessity of proving personal injury, it admits to no meaningful limit as to the behavior within its reach. Thus the state creates its own authority to act at will, by self-proxy-- where no authority to act by delegation exists. Which is to say, those in control of the state's power create-- all on their own-- new authority under which it will act, doing their will.

Partaking of the fiction of the magic sovereign is the philosophically complementary proposition that each and every person within the state's reach can be presumed, whether they acknowledge it or not, to have entered into an unwritten contract with it and owe it performance, which notion finds expression in the concepts of *duty to the state* and *offenses of omission*. Both are invoked heavily either directly or sub-textually in support of the "income" tax scheme that is our present focus, as well as for the justification of much other improper behavior by the state.

Another pernicious consequence of this construct is the recent trend toward direct adoption of its principles by various factions, in a bizarre balkanization of the polity into a multitude of magic sovereigns. So-called "hate crimes", which amount to the criminalizing of behavior causing no demonstrable harm to any individual but offending the sensibilities of a sub-community of identity-- according to its spokespeople-- serve as examples.

Whether the conduct being targeted (or demanded) through these legal and philosophical contortions is good or bad is not at all the point-- the point is the ugliness of narrow political interests adopting the mantle of an imaginary authority backed by all the vast power delegated to the state, for any purpose whatever.

2. Clarity of Command

A second essential element of proper law is clarity. Just as the delegation of authority must be explicit, so too must the product of the legislators to whom such delegations have been made. Clearly, no benefits over the soft and fuzzy admonitions of custom and tradition are extended by law which is ambiguous or subjective, or prone to constant interpretation and re-interpretation. Indeed, the entire purpose of law-making is to inform those to whom it applies precisely what is expected of them by others and how those others will formally react to any given behavior.

Law which can only be applied with the assistance of interpretation is therefore improper and void-- such law not only provides no usable notice of its requirements to those for whose interests it is purportedly crafted, but becomes necessarily the law of the interpreter rather than that of the delegatees. While an argument in defense of such free-form law has been advanced, to the effect that those delegatees are merely delegating authority in their turn, this proposition fails. Such delegatees do not have, and cannot delegate, such authority. Their only authority is what has been delegated to them, and they cannot be given the power of self-direction.

This is not to say that a delegation could not include the command that under this or that circumstance, and regarding this or that particular, law-making authority will pass to this or that other organ of the state. A command of this sort could even refer to this complication with language such as, "When such and such is the case, the legislature shall delegate law-making authority to the executive (or the judiciary)", although it would be an example of poor construction. What is really being said, however (the awkward language notwithstanding), is that when the specified circumstances obtain, the delegators withdraw the delegation from the legislature and grant it to the executive (or whoever) instead.

This principle is so elementary and fundamental that it needs no elaborate analysis. The law must mean what it says, and say what it means, or there is no purpose to it whatsoever. We do not establish a legislature, and delegate authority thereto, in order to guess at the meaning of its products or learn of their requirements and nuances only once charged with their violation, and in jeopardy of life, liberty or property.

Notably absent from our delegation of authority to the state is any providing that in cases in which the legislature should produce incomprehensible or even simply ambiguous "law", authority transfers to the judiciary under which that branch can "interpret" and "clarify" such flawed enactments. Judges are charged with the responsibility for overseeing the fair and proper enforcement of what the law IS, not of what it SHOULD be, or what they imagine the legislature must have meant. That the judiciary is empowered to rule an enactment unconstitutional is not an exception to this truth; such a ruling is no more than a declaration that the enactment in question either fails to provide clarity of command; exceeds delegated authority; or violates the requirements of proper notice (which we shall examine shortly). No law is thus promulgated by those to whom such authority has not been delegated. Sophomoric late-night-dorm-room protestations to the contrary notwithstanding, to say what something *isn't* does not amount to saying what it *is*, (which principle applies equally to the saying of what the delegated authority-- itself, by the way, also capable of insufficient clarity-- isn't).

Furthermore, the law must be expressed such that each participant can understand its requirements and nuances for themselves. No member of a society can properly be subject to the risks of being on the losing end of a conflict of interest with an interpreter, or be obliged to trade with an industry of translators in order to have explained what has been done with their own delegation of authority! The principle of rational self-interest precludes the legitimacy of such legislation, as much as does that of primary authority. That proper law is thus necessarily limited in both its scope and its depth is a facet of an elegant dynamic favoring the minimalist state.

There will, of course, always be some members of a society who cannot (or will not) comprehend some laws crafted by the associated state. Such persons cannot be viewed as having given their consent for those laws. They must be viewed as outside such laws. To the degree that such laws address transgressions against other members of society, non-consentors can be subject to their restraint-- the authority of self-defense thus exercised by those other members is unalienable and itself precedential to the state-- but cooperation with requirements-to-act (all versions of which amount to acts in support of the state), cannot properly be expected of them. No one can be legitimately enslaved to the interests of others, however untidy such a prohibition may seem. The practical application of this is that, once again, the state must remain small and simple.

Despite the obviousness of the principle of clarity of command, courtrooms across the United States are filled with defendants-- rich and poor alike-- being made to answer to a "law" which in many cases specifically excludes them from its ambit, but is deliberately written so as to encourage misunderstanding of this fact. Even more victims are held to account for requirements allegedly to be found among the incomprehensible hundreds of thousands of words of which many "laws", crafted to serve political rather than societal purposes, are made-- words which neither the judges, prosecutors, or defense attorneys could make even a credible pretense of having actually read.

3. Conformity to Established Procedures of Notice

The third pillar of legal propriety concerns the means by which the requirements of the law are made known to those on whom they will have effect. The legal cliché that, "Ignorance of the law is no excuse" can be true enough, but only where proper law prevails. Ignorance of a law passed in secret, or ambiguously crafted, is a complete and perfect excuse. No one can be held to account for a law the existence, meaning, or authority of which is kept from them, or is otherwise unavailable. Thus it is an essential principle that a consistent and effective means of notice be established and deployed.

As in all else regarding the law, ambiguity cannot be tolerated as to notice. A legitimate state will institute, and scrupulously abide by, explicit and well publicized rules for the construction, language, and dissemination of the law. (Indeed, no less than as regards clarity of meaning, a failure to do so must be viewed as an attempt to create a favored class within the greater host of participants, equipped with knowledge to be ransomed to their fellows.)

Laxness, even in the case of law related to the simplest and most common-sense behavior for which long and deeply established bodies of custom and tradition might exist, is unjustified and unacceptable. The necessity of rigid conformity to rules regarding form and notice is still more essential for statutes not enjoying such universal and instinctive embrace.

The very pinnacle of the importance of this principle attends statutes purporting to require positive action, as opposed to restraint. Such requirements are not natural to human interaction, and, unlike those imposing restraint, they involve no other interactive member whose competing interests an actor's behavior directly affects and who could therefore play a role in the notice process. (Restraints on purely private individual behavior are not under consideration here; they are all illegitimate.) The associated complications are undesirable, and fertile ground for misunderstanding and the development of intricate-- and therefore error-prone-- case law. Thus, it bears repeating: requirements of positive action under the law must be most scrupulously clear in authority, construction and notice.

The importance of respect for this principle, particularly as regards the element of clarity, can be illustrated by a look at America today. The mechanisms of proper form and notice are diligently provided for in the American legal structure, including two key elements in the United States Code:

> *Title 1, Chapter 2, Section 101- Enacting Clause: "The enacting clause of all Acts of Congress shall be in the following form: "Be it enacted by the Senate and House of Representatives of the United States of America in Congress assembled.'"*

and,

> *Title 5, Part 1, Chapter 5, Subchapter 2, Section 552- Public information; agency rules, opinions, orders, records, and proceedings:*
> *"(a) Each agency shall make available to the public information as follows:*
> *(1)(D) substantive rules of general applicability adopted as authorized by law, and statements of general policy or interpretations of general applicability formulated and adopted by the agency;"*

The US House of Representatives' Office of the Law Revision Counsel observes that of the 50 titles in the US Code, only 1, 3, 4, 5, 9, 10, 11, 13, 14, 17, 18, 23, 28, 31, 32, 35, 36, 37, 38, 39, 44, 46, and 49 have been enacted as positive law, leaving a 27 title majority both un-enacted, and often lacking published rules for significant sections.

Nonetheless, federal workers issue forth from high-rise fortresses throughout the country every morning to browbeat fines, plea bargains and concessions from citizens based upon those 27 titles, which consist largely of congressional declarations and executive orders, rather than statutes with general applicability. (At best, mere portions of those titles are distorted reflections of older actual statutes).

The fact is, those un-enacted titles are intermingled with the others, and within each type are intermingled in turn general statutes and the far more limited declarations and executive orders mentioned above, which only have application to federal entities or within federal territorial jurisdiction. This intermingling makes distinguishing each from the other extremely difficult-- effectively neutralizing the benefits of form and notice and leaving most Americans unable to challenge or resist illegitimate assertions of federal authority. The resultant passing of practical power from the citizenry to the state, by default rather than by consent, makes manifest the importance of respect for *all* the requirements of proper form and notice.

The chief object of the lawful state is to ensure domestic tranquility-- the kind of tranquility which results from the countless conflicts of a free and energetic society having reliable access to an impartial system of resolution and remedy. Such tranquility is not tidy, it is not quiet, and it is not ambitious. It is sheer, resting lightly upon all; and it is flexible, being constructed of values shared by the widest possible divergence of interests. It is as resilient as the laws of nature upon which it is based; and it is as beautiful as the aspirations of individual happiness cherished by each of those it protects. It yields great wealth and power to those who embrace it, but will abide only a light, sober and respectful embrace.

The founders of this great country drew up its plans in the illumination of their understanding of that tranquility and the engine that makes it possible: proper law. Only that particular radiance will reveal how the ongoing project can continue to fit together with the harmony and liberty which are its unique contribution to human weal. Arrogance, ambition, greed and fear all cast long shadows now, but the sharp lines of that great work of genius and humility are still there to be followed if such obstacles can be pushed aside. I hope we all find it in us to lend our weight to the task.

*****

Revenue acts, like any other legislative efforts, are either lawful or unlawful. If they say what they mean and mean what they say; are comprehensible without reliance on assumptions and inferences; and claim no authority not lawfully available, then they are lawful. If they do not mean what they say, or do not say what they mean, or claim authority not lawfully available, then they are unlawful, and void.

> *"The general rule is that an unconstitutional statute, though having the form and name of law, is in reality no law, but is wholly void, and ineffective for any purpose,*

> *since its unconstitutionality dates from the time of its enactment, and not merely from the date of the decision so branding it. [I]n legal contemplation, [it] is as inoperative as if it had never been passed... Since an unconstitutional law is void, the general principles follow that it imposes no duties, confers no rights, creates no office, bestows no power or authority on anyone, affords no protection, and justifies no acts performed under it... A void act cannot be legally consistent with a valid one. An unconstitutional law cannot operate to supersede any existing valid law. Indeed, insofar as a statute runs counter to the fundamental law of the land, it is superseded thereby. No one is bound to obey an unconstitutional law and no courts are bound to enforce it."* 16 Am Jur 2d page 177, section 256 (1979 ed.). Norton v. Shelby County, 118 U.S. 425

Federal revenue statutes are, in fact, lawful; but only due to the restrictions imposed by the plain meaning of the words with which they are constructed. Because of the manner in which those statutes are constructed, their sheer bulk, and the fact that those who benefit from a general public ignorance of the true nature of the tax vigorously promote a perception of ambiguity in their meaning where none really exists, the study and analysis of those statutes requires scrupulous parsing and careful attention to definitions and context.

As we proceed with that study, we will discover that anything which may initially appear to be ambiguous, or contrary to what we know about the law, resolves itself as we dig deeper. In the end, it will be clear that what the statutes DO actually say and mean is, in fact, confined to what they CAN say and mean-- as it must be, for were it otherwise, the statutes, and the authority they purport to exercise, would be inherently invalid.

The Plot Thickens

In 1921, after a bruising half-decade of corrective Supreme Court decisions among which were the Brushaber declaration that the "income tax" could only be sustained as an indirect excise; the So. Pacific v. Lowe ruling that "income" by which the tax could be measured had to amount to profit rather than simply receipts; and that of Eisner v. Macomber, 252 US 189 (1920), in which the court points out that,

> *"...it becomes essential to distinguish between what is, and what is not 'income'...Congress may not, by any definition it may adopt, conclude the matter, since it cannot by legislation alter the Constitution, from which alone it derives its power to legislate, and within whose limitations alone, that power can be lawfully exercised."*;

yet another Revenue Act issued forth from Congress, changing the previous version's language slightly:

> *Gross Income Defined:*
>
> *Section 213. That for the purposes of this title (except as otherwise provided in section 233* [Gross Income Of Corporations Defined -PH]*) the term gross income-*

> *(a) includes gains, profits, and income derived from salaries, wages, and compensation for personal service (including in the case of the President of the United States, the judges of the Supreme and inferior courts of the United States, and all other officers and employees, whether elected or appointed, of the United States, Alaska, Hawaii, or any political subdivision thereof, or the District of Columbia, the compensation received as such)...*

(The section goes on to list other sources from which *"gains, profits or income"* might be derived-- including the *"or derived from any source whatever"* language common to these acts.)

I suspect that it was after this enactment that Congress began to recognize the opportunities offered by craft in its statutory constructions. Doubtless the language in the section excerpted above led some of those new to the subject to presume that it purported to tax the compensation received by persons *not listed* within the parentheses as well as those who are. Such persons probably took it upon themselves to assess as taxable their own exempt private-sector and unprivileged compensation, and sent in a check to the treasury. (Happily, any confusion was not incredibly widespread. In a 1941 report titled "Collection at Source of the Individual Normal Income Tax", the Treasury Department's Division of Tax Research noted that,

> *"For 1936, taxable income tax returns filed represented only 3.9% of the population.",*

which percentage would have included all regular federal workers, PWA workers, ATF-license-holders, etc., along with any misled private persons. The same report also informs us that:

> *"The largest portion of consumer incomes in the United States is not subject to income taxation. Likewise, only a small proportion of the population of the United States is covered by the income tax.")*

Looking at the construction of the 1921 act by light of an informed perspective it is easy to see that the compensation-- the wages and salaries themselves, rather than a gain that might be derived from them through investment, etc.-- of certain persons is explicitly, and as an exception to the broader rule being promulgated, identified as being included in "income", just as it had been in the separate sections of the original 1862 act. Similarly, "income" for those not so explicitly and exceptionally identified is being confined to something 'derived' (and apart) from the wages, salaries, and compensation for personal service received by such persons. Otherwise it would just say, "*...(a) includes salaries, wages and compensation for personal services received by any person...*", or, at least, the parenthetic note would not be parenthetic and would read, *"among which salaries, wages and compensation shall also be included the compensation received by..."*.

Look carefully at the clearer version of this same statutory construction in the 1894 iteration previously excerpted in the discussion of the Pollock case:

> *Sec. 28. That in estimating the gains, profits and income* ***of any person*** *there shall be included...all other gains, profits, and income derived from any source whatever except that portion of the salary, compensation, or pay received for services in the civil, military, naval, or other service of the United States, including Senators, Representatives, and Delegates in Congress, from which the tax has been deducted"... "And provided further, That in cases where the salary or other compensation paid to any person in the employment or service of the United States shall not exceed the rate of four thousand dollars per annum, or shall be by fees, or uncertain or irregular in the amount or in the time during which the same shall have accrued or been earned,* ***such salary or other compensation shall be included in estimating the annual gains,***

> ***profits or income of the person to whom the same shall have been paid,*** *and shall include that portion of any income or salary upon which a tax has not been paid by the employer, where the employer is required by law to pay on the excess over four thousand dollars;*

(Such withholding from the pay of government workers over four thousand dollars is provided for further on in the act).

In this construction, again just as in the 1862 act, the "gains, profits and income *derived from* any source" by *any* person are to be included in estimating their total annual "gains, profits and income", but the compensation of federal workers is specifically identified as being *itself* included in the meaning of those words. The portion below $4000 is to be listed as "income" and self-assessed; that above $4000 is taxed at the source through withholding. The "compensation", etc., of private persons is clearly excluded by omission. Look again at the 1921 version:

> *Gross Income Defined:*
>
> *Section 213. That for the purposes of this title (except as otherwise provided in section 233* [Gross Income Of Corporations Defined -PH]*) the term gross income-*
>
> *(a) includes gains, profits, and income derived from salaries, wages, and compensation for personal service (including in the case of the President of the United States, the judges of the Supreme and inferior courts of the United States, and all other officers and employees, whether elected or appointed, of the United States, Alaska, Hawaii, or any political subdivision thereof, or the District of Columbia, the compensation received as such)... or all gains, profits and income derived from any source whatever."*

The only difference between the two is the misleading (and otherwise pointless) deliberate mention of unspecified *"salaries, wages and compensation for personal service"* as something from which *"gains, profits and income"* might be derived in the language of the 1921 act. (After all, *"gains, profits, and income derived from salaries, wages, and compensation for personal service"* is covered pretty thoroughly by *"all gains, profits and income derived from any source whatever."*.) There is no difference in the *meaning* of the two sections.

*****

By 1928 Congress abandons even the rudimentary and convoluted-- but still overt-- acknowledgements in the earlier acts, leaving entirely to the reader's knowledge of the law the distinction between the privileged, taxable compensation for services of government workers and that of unprivileged private-sector workers. The distinction still existed, of course-- the nature of the tax, and its limitations, were unchanged-- but there is no legal requirement to spell it out any more clearly.

The Revenue Act of 1928:

SEC. 22. GROSS INCOME.

(a) General definition.—"Gross income" includes gains, profits, and income derived from salaries, wages, or compensation for personal service, of whatever kind and in whatever form paid, or from professions, vocations, trades, businesses, commerce, or sales, or dealings in property, whether real or personal, growing out of the ownership or use of or interest in such property; also from interest, rent, dividends, securities, or the transaction of any business carried on for gain or profit, or gains or profits and income derived from any source whatever.

In all fairness, it must be acknowledged that between the 1921 act and that of 1928, Congress had enacted the 'Classification Act of 1923', in which a number of custom terms were created and defined. The existence of this act mitigates what otherwise would appear to be a more brazen attempt at congressional obfuscation in the sparser construction of the 1928 version. Everyone, after all, is legally presumed to be keeping themselves up-to-date with all these details.

Here is the act with relevant language emphasized:

The Classification Act of 1923

42 Stat. 1488

March 4, 1923

[H.R. 8928]

[Public, No. 516]

CHAP. 265.--An Act To provide for the classification of ***civilian positions within the District of Columbia and in the field services.***

Be it enacted by the Senate and House of Representatives of the United States of America in Congress assembled, That this Act may be cited as "The Classification Act of 1923."

SEC. 2. That the term "compensation schedules" means the schedules of positions, grades, and salaries, as contained in section 13 of the Act.

The term "department" means an executive department of the United States Government, a governmental establishment in the executive branch of the United States Government which is not a part of an executive department, the municipal government of the District of Columbia, the Botanic Garden, Library of Congress, Library Building and Grounds, Government Printing Office, and the Smithsonian Institution.

The term "the head of the department" means the officer or group of officers in the department who are not subordinate or responsible to any other officer of the department.

The term "board" means the Personal Classification Board established by section 3 hereof.

*The term **"position"** means a specific civilian office or employment, whether occupied or vacant, in a department other than the following: Offices or employments in the Postal Service; teachers, librarians, school attendance officers, and employees of the community center department under the Board of Education of the District of Columbia; officers and members of the Metropolitan police, the fire department of the District of Columbia, and the United States park police; and the commissioned personnel of the Coast Guard, the Public Health Service, and the Coast and Geodetic Survey.*

*The term **"employee"** means any person temporarily or permanently in a position.*

*The term **"service"** means the broadest division of related offices and employments.*

The term "grade" means a subdivision of a service, including one or more positions for which approximately the same basic qualifications and compensation are prescribed, the distinction between grades being based upon differences in the importance, difficulty, responsibility, and value of the work.

The term "class" means a group of positions to be established under this Act sufficiently similar in respect to the duties and responsibilities thereof that the same requirements as to education, experience, knowledge, and ability are demanded of incumbents, and the same schedule of compensation is made to apply with equity.

*The term **"compensation" means any salary, wage, fee, allowance, or other emolument paid to an employee for service in a position.***

[The remainder of the act is omitted.]

The existence of the Classification Act may have helped Congress feel excused from the necessity of greater clarity in the 1928 act and the several similar revenue acts that succeeded it. After all, though much better concealed under the new protocol, the "income" derived from "compensation" (as defined in the Classification Act) still amounts to the value of every dollar paid as such "compensation".

The Classification Act of 1923 was replaced in 1949 with an updated version making minor changes-- The Classification Act of 1949 (now codified in Title 5 of the USC). The qualifying effects of these acts were incorporated into the relevant sections of all revenue statutes passed from the original act's inception onward and thus into the Internal Revenue Codes, as well (which are nothing more than a representation of such statutes, as we will discuss thoroughly in a little while).

This effect is particularly important in clarifying the representations in the modern Section 61 of the IRC, *'Gross Income Defined'*, and its inclusion of *'compensation for services'* after the deployment of the general language: *"[G]ross income means all income from whatever source derived, including (but not limited to) the following items:"*. Legislative notes regarding the construction of that code section also clarify its meaning, and the consistency of the current version of the law with the earlier enactments. As is noted on page A19 of 'House Report No. 1337: Internal Revenue Code of 1954, Report of the Committee on Ways and Means, House of Representatives, to accompany H.R. 8300, 'A Bill to Revise the Internal Revenue Laws of the United States",

> *"After the general definition [in section 61(a)] there has been included, for purposes of illustration, an enumeration of 15 of the more common items constituting gross income."*

The Law Means What It Says

Introduction

(1) Our system of taxation is dependent on taxpayers' belief that the tax laws they follow apply to everyone and that the Internal Revenue Service will respect and protect their rights under the law. These are fundamental principles of voluntary compliance.

Internal Revenue Manual, Part 5, Collection Activity 105.4.1.2 (07/27/98)

"Inclusio unius est exclusio alterius. The inclusion of one is the exclusion of another. The certain designation of one person is an absolute exclusion of all others. ... This doctrine decrees that where law expressly describes [a] particular situation to which it shall apply, an irrefutable inference must be drawn that what is omitted or excluded was intended to be omitted or excluded."

Black's Law Dictionary, 6th edition.

It is axiomatic (and the law) that terms and phrases within a statute for which definitions are provided DO NOT have their common meanings as used therein.

"The [state supreme] court also considered that the word 'including' was used as a word of enlargement, the learned court being of the opinion that such was its ordinary sense. With this we cannot concur."
U.S. Supreme Court, Montello Salt Co. v. Utah, 221 U.S. 452 (1911)

I mentioned in the foreword to this book that for decades efforts to mis-apply the income tax to receipts connected with private-sector activities have capitalized upon the widespread presumption that despite no one ever *seeing* it, some portion of the law *must* explicitly impose the tax upon them. Any who have questioned this presumption have been treated by defenders of the scheme to a little maze of circular arguments revolving around the term "includes", of which we will see a great deal as we move forward into examination of the nuts-and-bolts of the "income" tax laws. The real essence of this effort is to wear down the questioner; it offers nothing but suggested implications about other parts of the law to answer that fatal central doubt, but it is the best the schemers can do.

The principles discussed earlier in 'Regarding the Law and Its Virtues' should make addressing this nonsense unnecessary; however, it must be acknowledged that the construction of the relevant portions of the law combines sufficiently with a lifelong misinformation campaign regarding this subject to nurture a somewhat forgivable uncertainty in some. This is particularly true in light of the bellicose demeanor of those who benefit from that doubt-- it is a natural human reaction to seize upon, and not examine too closely, an even marginally plausible justification for declining to confront a snarling, rabid animal such as the IRS.

Here is the dodge: The tax laws very studiously and deliberately deploy terms with unique, custom definitions, such as "employee", "trade or business" and "United States". That these terms mimic normal words is itself confusing, and would itself be sufficient to quiet many objectors, particularly those who never go so far as to discover their custom-definitions (which is to say, most). At this level, inquiry ceases when confronted with, for instance, *"The law says "everyone engaged in a trade or business shall..."*.

Deeper inquiry, by which the custom meaning of key terms is revealed, is more problematic to the tax scheme, but those clarifying definitions have themselves an obfuscating element seized upon by its beneficiaries. Whether by craft or simple bureaucratic awkwardness, many of these definitions incorporate the term "includes", as in *(26) Trade or business: The term "trade or business" includes the performance of the functions of a public office.* At this level of inquiry the skeptical are encouraged to imagine that the use of "includes" indicates that things outside the scope of the custom definition provided are incorporated within its meaning as well, by implication.

Finally, in the face of a refusal to accept the imposition of law to "implied" subjects, the beneficiaries of the scheme roll out mirrors to supplement the smoke and direct the insistent doubter's attention to the custom definition of "includes" provided within the code (in section 7701(c)): *"Includes and including: The terms "includes" and "including" when used in a definition contained in this title shall not be deemed to exclude other things otherwise within the meaning of the term defined."*

This is the eight-hundred-pound gorilla of obfuscation available to the "income" tax schemers. Presented within the context described, it is meant to suggest a sort of legal foundation for the imposition of the law by implication rather than specification. Really, as thus used, it's just an elaborate formulation of the age-old legal maxim, *"Because I said so!"* The intended misunderstanding of the section is that terms defined as *"xx includes..."* embrace all things commonly meant by the *word* being custom re-defined plus those things listed after *"includes"*-- but again, *merely by implication*. Happily, this effort to muddy the waters quickly fails under analysis. As we are about to delve into the morass of these mis-directions, it behooves us to undertake that exercise.

(There may be some who will feel that I devote more attention to this one little word than seems reasonable. However, in light of the fact that all but a truly rarefied few private-sector persons have lost possession of at least 15% of their earnings each and every working year of their lives the diversion of which has been justified solely by a cunning misconstruction of this little word, I respectfully disagree.)

To start with, we must recognize that if a word is meant to be understood as having its common meaning, there is no need to define it at all. It is axiomatic that if a word *is* explicitly defined, it has a restricted meaning. If language such as, *"For purposes of this paragraph, the term "Fruit" includes apples, pears, and oranges."* is used, it can only be understood as restricting the definition to those things listed, or no definition would be required; the word *"fruit"* would be understood to include apples, pears and oranges, as well as all other fruits.

Second, note that the word *"common"* (or its equivalent) is left out of the definition of *"includes"* and *"including"*, creating a sophomoric circular argument. The only *"other things otherwise within the meaning of the term defined"* are those that are the same as those used to provide the definition. In other words, the *"things"* used in the definition are what establish the class to which the *"other things"* must belong in order to be included under the doctrine of 7701(c), and, as the word is being deliberately defined, the common meaning of the word must be excluded.

To see what I mean, insert the word *"common"* as follows: *"The terms "includes" and "including" when used in a definition contained in this title shall not be deemed to exclude other things otherwise with the common meaning of the term defined."*. Without it, the section is meaningless, but misleading, as intended; and furthermore, note that the statute says, *"...the meaning of the **term** defined."*, rather than the **word** defined. If Congress had meant (and been Constitutionally able) to embrace within its definitions the *common* meaning of the words being made into legal terms it would have written 7701(c) in that way: *"The terms "includes" and "including" when used in a definition contained in this title shall not be deemed to exclude other things otherwise within the common meaning of the word defined."* The *word* isn't a *term* until the provided definition has been applied, at which point its common meaning has been stripped away.

Properly understood, 7701(c) declares that, *"Includes and including: The terms "includes" and "including" when used in a definition contained in this title shall not be deemed to exclude other things otherwise within the meaning of the term* ***as*** *defined."* Indeed, at one time there was a regulatory clarification of the 7701(c) definition of "includes" in 26 CFR which clearly embraced this construction (unsurprisingly long since deleted and not replaced):

> *26 CFR 170.59- Meaning of Terms: The terms "includes and including" do not exclude things not enumerated which are in the same general class.*

The accuracy of these points is established by more than simple logic and the inadvertent forthrightness of a one-time bureaucrat (doubtless fired for his blunder). Ask yourself this: If *"Fruit"* is defined as, *"When used in this paragraph, the term "Fruit" includes turnips, carrots and broccoli."*, is it to be presumed that the term also means apples? How about if in the next paragraph one finds, *"For purposes of this paragraph the term "Fruit" includes apples, turnips, carrots and broccoli."* Should it be presumed that apples was included by implication in the first definition and the writer was just lazy, or ran out of typewriter ribbon? Obviously not. (If the writer had, in the first instance, said, *"For purposes of this paragraph the term "Fruit", in addition to the commonly understood meaning of the word "fruit", includes..."* or, *"..."Fruit", in addition to all fruits, includes..."* or even simply, *"..."Fruit" also includes..."*, all is different. But he did not.) No less an authority than the United States Supreme Court reminds us to refrain from reading anything into a statute when Congress has left it out:

> *" '[W]here Congress includes particular language in one section of a statute but omits it in another ..., it is generally presumed that Congress acts intentionally and purposely in the disparate inclusion or exclusion.' "* Russello v. United States, 464 US 16, 23, 78 L Ed 2d 17, 104 S Ct. 296 (1983) (Quoting United States v. Wong Kim Bo, 472 F. 2d 720, 722 (CA 1972))

As previously noted, some of the key definitions upon which the broadest misapplication of the law are based (regarding "wages", in this example) involve the custom legal meaning of terms like "employee", "employer" and "United States" as used in the law and reproduced in the code (all of which we will discuss in detail shortly). These sections read as follows:

> *3401(c) Employee*
> *For purposes of this chapter, the term "employee" includes an officer, employee, or elected official of the United States, a State, or any political subdivision thereof, or the District of Columbia, or any agency or instrumentality of any one or more of the foregoing. The term "employee" also includes an officer of a corporation.*

3401(d) Employer
For purposes of this chapter, the term "employer" means the person for whom an individual performs or performed any service, of whatever nature, as the employee [as defined above -PH] *of such person...*

and:

3121(e)(2) United States
The term "United States" when used in a geographical sense includes the Commonwealth of Puerto Rico, the Virgin Islands, Guam, and American Samoa.

Now, keeping in mind the declaration by the Supreme Court in Russello (and our logical analysis), look at the following definitions in the U.S code which *are not* relied upon to mislead (at least not for the same purposes or in the same way as their counterparts which are the subjects of our discussion), and recognize that when Congress means to legislate broadly, it plainly says so:

Title 26, Subtitle D, Chapter 38, Subchapter A, Sec. 4612. [Petroleum Tax] *For purposes of this subchapter-*
(4) United States
In general
The term "United States" means the 50 States, the District of Columbia, the Commonwealth of Puerto Rico, any possession of the United States, the Commonwealth of the Northern Mariana Islands, and the Trust Territory of the Pacific Islands.

and also,

Title 20, Chapter 69, Section 6103 (Education)
As used in this chapter:
(8) Employer- The term "employer" includes both public and private employers.

Clearly, even if one were to be generous in interpreting 7701(c)'s definition of *"includes and including"* and grant it the effect of limited expansion assumed under the old regulatory clarification to which I previously referred, (and which is, by the way, still deployed in the regulations for Title 27, at 27 CFR 72.11):

> *Meaning of Terms: The terms "includes and including" do not exclude things not enumerated which are in the same general class,*

that effect does not bring non-federal persons and places into the ambit of the terms we are discussing. Instead, the most that could be said in that regard is that in addition to the listed varieties, "employee" in Section 3401 also refers to other federally-connected workers whose descriptions are not specifically listed (and "employer" the agencies for which they work); and that "United States", as used in 3121, can be understood to include other federal territories and possessions similarly left off the enumerated list.

In fact, this is the only construction consistent with the relevant doctrines expressed by the United States Supreme Court as:

> *"[W]here general words follow specific words in a statutory enumeration, the general words are construed to embrace only objects similar in nature to those objects enumerated by the preceding specific words"* Circuit City Stores v. Adams, 532 US 105, 114-115 (2001),

> *"Under the principle of ejusdem generis, when a general term follows a specific one, the general term should be understood as a reference to subjects akin to the one with specific enumeration."* Norfolk & Western R. Co. v. Train Dispatchers, 499 US 117 (1991),

and

> *"...a word is known by the company it keeps (the doctrine of noscitur a sociis). This rule we rely upon to avoid ascribing to one word a meaning so broad that it is inconsistent with its accompanying words, thus giving*

"unintended breadth to the Acts of Congress." Jarecki v. G. D. Searle & Co., 367 US 303, 307 (1961)" Gustafson v. Alloyd Co. (93-404), 513 US 561 (1995).

Applying these principles of statutory construction, we see that the language of 26 USC 7701(c) providing for the inclusion of "things otherwise within the meaning of the term defined" effectively constitutes the "general words", or "general term" referred to by the Supreme Court in the Circuit City and Norfolk & Western rulings, which are then followed by the specifically enumerated things listed in the given definition. Look again the definition of "employee" at 26 USC 3401(c):

> *For purposes of this chapter, the term "employee" includes an officer, employee, or elected official of the United States, a State, or any political subdivision thereof, or the District of Columbia, or any agency or instrumentality of any one or more of the foregoing. The term "employee" also includes a [paid] officer of a corporation.* [meaning a "United States" corporation only, by the way-- more on that and the "paid" thing later in 'Withholding The Truth'...]

It is clear that the common characteristic of those in the enumerated list of "employees" in this special definition is that of being someone paid by the federal government (or an entity created and/or controlled by the federal government) for services rendered.

When we proceed to incorporate the provisions of 7701(c) (as properly illuminated by the doctrines outlined above) we get:

> *For purposes of this chapter, the term "employee" includes an officer, employee, or elected official of the United States, a State, or any political subdivision thereof, or the District of Columbia, or any agency or instrumentality of any one or more of the foregoing. The term "employee" also includes an officer of a*

corporation. The term "employee" also includes "things not enumerated which are in this same general class" (that is, "other things otherwise within the meaning of the term as defined").

No further expansion can be admitted:

"It is axiomatic that the statutory definition of the term excludes unstated meanings of that term." U.S. Supreme Court, Meese v. Keene, 481 U.S. 465 (1987)

Finally, though it is irrelevant to the logical analysis of section 7701(c) (other than to underscore its relevant meaninglessness), it's worth observing that a declaration that SOME thing(s) shall not be deemed to be *excluded* does not mean that any particular thing must or should be deemed to be *included*-- especially when what we are encouraged to ASSUME is meant to be included could easily have been explicitly provided for. After all, what 7701(c) DOESN'T say is, *"Includes and including: The terms "includes" and "including" when used in a definition contained in this title shall be construed as expanding the class represented by the common meaning of the word defined with the addition of the explicitly listed items."*-- language by which Congress could have avoided a lot of confusion if this is what it actually meant.

For that matter, Congress could have simply defined "includes" and "including" in the tax law as expressly non-limiting, as it has done elsewhere:

28 USC 3003- Rules of Construction

(a) For purposes of this chapter

(1) the terms "includes" and "including" are not limiting;

and,

11 USC 102- Rules of Construction

In this title-

...

(3) "includes" and "including" are not limiting.

That it did not must be given proper significance. As the United States Supreme Court observes,

> *"The construction of a statute by those charged with its execution should be followed unless there are compelling indications that it is wrong, especially when Congress has refused to alter the administrative construction, and such deference is particularly appropriate where an agency's interpretation involves issues of considerable public controversy and Congress has not acted to correct any misperception of its statutory objectives."* CBS, INC. v FCC, 453 US 367 (1981)

The existing language has been on the books for more than 79 years, and Congress has revised the law, the code, and the related regulations many, many times during that period.

The IRS has floated a ridiculous "supporting explanation" of all this to the effect that the use of *"includes [whatever]"* in key places in the code is because of doubts at one time as to whether public-sector entities were covered by the IRC. This proposition might have a little hang time if the relevant references were found in an addendum or supplement (and if it could be credibly asserted that anyone would otherwise have doubted that, for instance, the guy sorting mail at the Senate Office Building is an employee within the common meaning of the word), but not when they constitute the sole definition of the term. There IS no other list to which the public-sector references can be added; they ARE the list, and they have been since 1862. (The IRS doesn't attempt to explain why, if what it suggests is true, Congress didn't spare us our doubts and simply add one little section applying to the whole code saying, *"Public sector workers, officials and organizations are to be considered subject to the requirements of this title in the same fashion as are private citizens and organizations."*.)

For example, although originally introduced in section 86 of the Revenue Act of 1862, the "wage" withholding specified in that section was abandoned early in the 20th century. The practice was re-introduced by way of the Current Tax Payment Act of 1943 on June 9, 1943. The definition of "employee" which we have been discussing on the preceding pages is taken from that act. The act provided for an addition to chapter 9 of the IRC of 1939 code of what later became codified as subchapter 24 of the current IRC, with the "employee" definition denominated as subparagraph (c) of section 1641.

Material related to the new act was promptly published in the Federal Register, as is the case with all such enactments. Here is how the "employee" definition is described in the register edition of Tuesday, September 7, 1943 (page 12267):

> *SUBCHAPTER D-- COLLECTION OF INCOME TAX AT SOURCE OF WAGES*
>
> *SEC. 1621. DEFINITIONS*
> *As used in this subchapter--*
>
> * * * * *
>
> *(c) Employee. The term "employee includes an officer, employee, or elected official of the United States, a State, Territory, or any political subdivision thereof, or the District of Columbia, or any agency or instrumentality of any one or more of the foregoing. The term "employee" also includes an officer of a corporation.*
>
> * * * * *
>
> *§ 404.104 Employee. The term "employee" includes every individual performing services if the relationship between him and the person for whom he performs such services is the legal relationship of employer and employee. The term specifically includes officers and employees whether elected or appointed, of the United*

> *States, a State, Territory, or any political subdivision thereof, or the District of Columbia, or any agency or instrumentality of any one or more of the foregoing.*

Plainly, this definition has always covered federal workers as discussed above, and only such workers. Plainly, not only is "includes" NOT deployed in this definition in order to ADD federal workers to anything, but there WAS no previously operating definition or withholding protocol of this kind to which they could be added.

The simple, tawdry fact is that Congress wants to spend lots of your money-- and even though it can't seize that money from you legally, it is perfectly willing to set up a system by which you are led to believe that it can, and about which you will have great difficulty discovering the truth. Dwell on this a while and the nuances of the phrase "voluntary compliance" will suddenly become clear. What it refers to is you "voluntarily" allowing yourself to be characterized as a recipient of public-sector privilege, and then complying with requirements that attach to that status.

From about this point on, we're going to be reading a fair bit of the Internal Revenue Code. As we do, ask yourself, *"Why is it written like this? Is it written like this because it means what its beneficiaries want me to believe that it means, or is it written like this because it doesn't mean what its beneficiaries want me to believe that it means?"*

Recognize that it is no coincidence that at every point in the code where Congress would clearly be exceeding its lawful authority if the section meant what it is hoped you will *think* it means, a key *apparent* ambiguity makes an appearance. Suddenly, at such points, we see "includes" in a definition that

conveniently fails to mention or comprehend private citizens; or vague, complicated references to those "made liable" similarly shy of inconvenient, clarifying details. Suddenly there will be a confusion of references to other sections and subsections, and elaborate qualifiers and modifiers running hundreds or thousands of words in which the one pertinent element is buried. Keep this in mind, and don't be fooled.

*****

"When the words of a statute are unambiguous, the first canon of statutory construction [that courts must presume that a legislature says in a statute what it means and means in a statute what it says there] is also the last, and judicial inquiry is complete." United States Supreme Court, Connecticut National Bank v. Germain, 503 US 249 (1992)

(For that matter, even when the words of a tax-related statute DO happen to be ambiguous:

> *"In the interpretation of statutes levying taxes it is the established rule not to extend their provisions, by implication, beyond the clear import of the language used, or to enlarge their operations so as to embrace matters not specifically pointed out. In case of doubt they are construed most strongly against the government, and in favor of the citizen."* United States Supreme Court, Gould v. Gould, 245 US 151 (1917)...)

Now, on to the Code...

The Code Is Born

On February 10th, 1939, the first Internal Revenue Code was published. It was mostly just a compilation of all revenue acts then in force. Any changes in the language of those earlier acts resulting from that compiling (which were myriad) were not enacted into law. Consequently, except where subsequent formal enactments have explicitly amended or otherwise modified language found therein, such language is subordinate to the older, original laws. This is very significant, because in constructing the code (and the revised code of 1954, and that of 1986) the best that can be said is that a game of post-office is being played, with each reiteration of the original and still dominant law becoming less accurate in its communication of that law. A less charitable view would imagine this process to be deliberate. The misleading disconnectedness from the actual requirements of the law becomes even more pronounced in the regulations associated with each code. However, in the preface to the IRC of 1939, describing its nature as a compilation, we find the following:

> "*The internal revenue title, which comprises all of the Code except the preliminary sections relating to its*

enactment, is intended to contain all the United States statutes of a general and permanent nature relating exclusively to internal revenue, in force on January 2, 1939; also such of the temporary statutes of that description as relate to taxes the occasion of which may arise after the enactment of the Code. These statutes are codified without substantive change and with only such change of form as is required by arrangement and consolidation. The title contains no provision, except for effective date, not derived from a law approved prior to January 3, 1939... The whole body of internal revenue law in effect on January 2, 1939, therefore, has its ultimate origin in 164 separate enactments of Congress. The earliest of these was approved July 1, 1862; the latest, June 16, 1938...."

and within the code, we find this:

Sec. 7806. - Construction of title

(b) Arrangement and classification

No inference, implication, or presumption of legislative construction shall be drawn or made by reason of the location or grouping of any particular section or provision or portion of this title, nor shall any table of contents, table of cross references, or similar outline, analysis, or descriptive matter relating to the contents of this title be given any legal effect.

(In other words, just because in assembling one big mock-up of a few hundred actual laws we may have obscured the legal requirements reflected therein, don't make the mistake of thinking that those requirements have changed.)

The "definition of gross income" section of the 1939 compilation was drawn from the 1938 act, and read as follows:

Section 22(a): Gross income includes gains, profits, and income derived from salaries, wages, or compensation for personal service, of

> *whatever kind and in whatever form paid, or from professions, vocations, trades, businesses, commerce, or sales, or dealings in property, whether real or personal; also from interest, rent, dividends, securities, or the transaction of any business carried on for gains or profits, or gains or profits from any source whatever.*

Two months after the release of the code, the Public Salary Tax Act of 1939 was enacted -- extending application of the "income" tax to the government workers of U.S. possessions and providing, among other things, for reciprocal taxation of federal, District of Columbia, and U.S. possessions government employees by each respective institution. The new act contained the following element:

> *SECTION 1. Section 22 (a) of the Internal Revenue Code (relating to the definition of "gross income") is amended by inserting after the words "compensation for personal service" the following: ("including personal service as an officer or employee of a State, or any political subdivision thereof, or any agency or instrumentality of the foregoing).*

(Needless to say, the federal government has no authority to subject officers and employees of the several union States to taxation by decree. In fact, such a thing is explicitly prohibited as a violation of sovereignty. The key to this puzzle is section 7701, at which we looked a bit in 'The Law Means What It Says'. There we find the sometimes startlingly contrary-to-common-usage definitions of many of the custom terms found throughout the code. The definition provided there in paragraph (10) applies to the language above:

> *(10) State*
> *The term "State" shall be construed to include the District of Columbia, where such construction is*

necessary to carry out provisions of this title. [as in, to keep it Constitutional],

as does the language in the following section:

Sec. 7651. - Administration and collection of taxes in possessions

(1) Applicability of administrative provisions

All provisions of the laws of the United States applicable to the assessment and collection of any tax imposed by this title or of any other liability arising under this title (including penalties) shall, in respect of such tax or liability, extend to and be applicable in any possession of the United States in the same manner and to the same extent as if such possession were a State, and as if the term "United States" when used in a geographical sense included such possession.)

I mention this act both because the portion reproduced above finds its way into section 3401 of the IRC, a section with which we will be particularly concerned shortly; and because it is instructive in itself. Those still unconvinced that everything they have previously been led to believe about the "income" tax is wrong should be very troubled by the Public Salary Tax Act. After all, if *everybody's* pay amounts to part of the *"gains, profits and income"* upon which tax must be paid, then that of *"an officer or employee of a State, or any political subdivision thereof, or any agency or instrumentality of the foregoing"* was already covered by earlier *"any person"* and *"...from whatever source derived"* language before they were added to the list by the act, making that part of it pointless... right?

The Public Salary Tax Act emphasizes that unless specifically enumerated within the language of a statute, that left out is not covered. Congress had always had the power to tax any federal privilege beneficiary; it had simply chosen not to tax these ones in the past. The act added the *"compensation for personal service"* of "State" (U.S. possessions) workers (still operating under the definitions in the Classification Act of 1923, by the way) to the category of benefits-of-privilege explicitly identified as being themselves directly of the nature of *"gains, profits and income"*, just as that of federal government workers has always been since the inception of "income" taxation, and that of District of Columbia government workers since 1921.

Today's version of section 22(a) has dropped the explicit reference to the workers added in the Public Salary Tax Act as no longer needing to be restated, just as the 1928 and subsequent acts stopped mentioning federal officers and employees and District of Columbia workers:

> *Sec. 61. - Gross income defined*
>
> *(a) General definition*
>
> > *Except as otherwise provided in this subtitle, gross income means all income from whatever source derived, including (but not limited to) the following items:*
>
> *(1)*
>
> > *Compensation for services, including fees, commissions, fringe benefits, and similar items;*
> >
> > ...

The doctrine is simple and standard in statutory construction: when an element of a statute has once been promulgated, it remains the law, whether spelled out in a future version or not, unless explicitly repealed.

However, the distinction of the pay, in particular, of federal, D.C. and "State" government workers as being-- unlike private-sector workers-- of the character of *"gains, profits, and income"* is still exhibited clearly in the withholding provisions of the revenue law. Those provisions, having been rearranged, and amended per section 1 of the Public Salary Tax Act, reappeared in section 466 of the Revenue Act of 1942 in the form we know today, and then were relocated again in the IRC of 1954 to their present resting place in Subtitle C.

Withholding The Truth

By the time the Current Tax Payment Act of 1943 reiterated the withholding-from-pay provisions first spelled out in the Act of 1862 (and expanded their application to "State" workers, per the Public Salary Tax Act), the people writing these acts had become very accustomed to living large, and had a good handle on how their bread was being buttered. They had learned that ambiguities in the language of tax statutes combined productively (from their viewpoint) with a general weakness in legal literacy among the lay population.

It had also not escaped their attention that the lawyers and other specialists upon whom most of that lay population, business owners included, relied for expertise were making good livings dishing it out solely due to the complexity of the code. They were generally happy enough to go along and get along, if provided at least a fig-leaf of semantic cover with which to shield themselves from malpractice risks.

Furthermore, and in, I suppose, their defense, the legislative draftsmen charged with the modern tax code were cognizant that:

> *"Words having universal scope, such as 'every contract in restraint of trade,' 'every person who shall monopolize,' etc., will be taken, as a matter of course, to mean only everyone subject to such legislation, not all that the legislator subsequently may be able to catch."* United States Supreme Court, American Banana Co. v. United Fruit Co., 213 U.S. 347 (1909)

It is to their credit that these bureaucrats and staffers did not take full advantage of the latitude to which they were technically entitled by virtue of rulings such as this. They could have left to every litigant or judge complete responsibility for understanding, calculating and invoking the limits imposed on every statute by its context. Instead, in many instances the legislative draftsmen spelled out the limitations of their product for the truly diligent researcher to uncover. Nonetheless, in crafting the new wording of the same old provisions for withholding from the pay of federal-connected workers, they tried to make it tough, particularly by use of the term "includes".

> Here is the original language again:
> *"and it shall be the duty of all paymasters, and all disbursing officers, under the government of the United States, or in the employ thereof, when making any payments to officers and persons as aforesaid, or upon settling and adjusting the accounts of such officers and persons, to deduct and withhold the aforesaid duty of three per centum, and shall, at the same time, make a certificate stating the name of the officer or person from whom such deduction was made, and the amount thereof, which shall be transmitted to the office of the Commissioner of Internal Revenue, and entered as part of the internal duties;... Section 86, Revenue Act of 1862*
> Here is what appears to be the current version:
> *Sec. 3402. - Income tax collected at source*

(a) Requirement of withholding

(1) In general

*Except as otherwise provided in this section, every employer making payment of **wages** shall deduct and withhold upon such wages a tax determined in accordance with tables or computational procedures prescribed by the Secretary. Any tables or procedures prescribed under this paragraph shall-...*

At first glance, that sounds as though it covers everybody, doesn't it? After all, 'wages' is widely used as a generic word for 'pay', (much like the way 'income' is widely used for 'all that comes in'). However, looking a little deeper into the bowels of this subchapter, we find:

Sec. 3401. - Definitions

*(a) **Wages***

*For purposes of this chapter, the term "wages" means all remuneration (other than fees paid to a public official) for services performed by an **employee** for his employer,...*

*(c) **Employee***

***For purposes of this chapter, the term "employee" includes an officer, employee, or elected official of the United States, a State, or any political subdivision thereof, or the District of Columbia, or any agency or instrumentality of any one or more of the foregoing. The term "employee" also includes an officer of a corporation**.* [A "United States Corporation", defined in Sec. 207 of the Public Salary Tax Act as, *"a corporate agency or instrumentality, is one (a) a majority of the stock of which is owned by or on behalf of the United States, or (b) the power to appoint or select a majority of the board of directors of which is exercisable by or on*

> *behalf of the United States...".* However, we are instructed by the IRS in Pub. 15A that such officers are only to be considered "employees" if they are paid as a consequence of their positions.]
>
> *(d) Employer*
>
> *For purposes of this chapter, the term "employer" means the person for whom an individual performs or performed any service, of whatever nature, as the* ***employee*** *of such person...*

So, actually, this kind of withholding only applies to the pay of federal government workers, exactly as it always has (plus "State" government workers, since 1939, and those of the District of Columbia since 1921). Remember the inclusion - exclusion rule: Where the remuneration (compensation) of one group is explicitly identified as an object of the law-- whether for withholding or as "income", or in any other respect-- the remuneration of an omitted group is explicitly excluded as an object of that law. Think of it this way: The Selective Service Act says (more or less), *"All male citizens of the United States, upon reaching the age of eighteen, shall register...".* Has your Aunt Sophie ever queued up? Would she if the law were re-constructed as follows?

> *(a) Draft Registration Required:*
>
> > *All citizens shall register for the draft upon reaching eighteen years of age.*
>
> *(b) Definitions:*
>
> > *As used in paragraph (a), the term "citizens" includes male citizens of the United States.*

How about if it were like this?

> *(a) Draft Registration Required:*
>
> > *All citizens shall register for the draft.*
>
> *(b) Definitions:*

> *As used in paragraph (a), the term "citizens" includes male citizens of the United States having reached the age of eighteen.*

Of course not.

Let's look at the more trickily constructed, but, at bottom, similarly restricted application of FICA (Federal Insurance Contributions Act-- Social Security and Medicaid) taxes:

> *Sec. 3101. - Rate of tax*
> *(a) Old-age, survivors, and disability insurance*
> *In addition to other taxes, there is hereby imposed on the income of every individual a tax equal to the following percentages of the* ***wages*** *(as defined in section 3121(a)) received by him with respect to* ***employment*** *(as defined in section 3121(b))...*
>
> *Sec. 3121. - Definitions*
> *(a)* ***Wages***
> *For purposes of this chapter, the term "wages" means all remuneration for* ***employment****, including the cash value of all remuneration (including benefits) paid in any medium other than cash; except that such term shall not include - ...* [various pre-tax deductions]
> *(b)* ***Employment***
> *For purposes of this chapter, the term "employment" means any* ***service****, of whatever nature, performed*
>
> > *(A) by an employee for the person employing him, irrespective of the citizenship or residence of either,*
> >
> > > *(i)* ***within the United States****, or*
> > > *(ii) on or in connection with an American vessel or American aircraft... or*

(B) outside the United States by a ***citizen or resident of the United States*** *as an employee for an* ***American employer*** *(as defined in subsection (h)),...*

(e) State, United States, and [Puerto Rican] *citizen*
For purposes of this chapter -

(1) State
The term "State" includes the District of Columbia, the Commonwealth of Puerto Rico, the Virgin Islands, Guam, and American Samoa.

(2) United States
The term "United States" ***when used in a geographical sense*** *includes the Commonwealth of Puerto Rico, the Virgin Islands, Guam, and American Samoa.*

...

h) ***American employer***
For purposes of this chapter, the term "American employer" means an employer which is -

(1) the United States or any instrumentality thereof,
(2) an individual who is a ***resident*** *of the United States,*
(3) a partnership, if two-thirds or more of the partners are ***residents*** *of the United States,*
(4) a trust, if all of the trustees are ***residents*** *of the United States, or*
(5) a corporation organized under the laws of the United States or of any State.

So, though more complicated than the withholding provisions in 3401, when read carefully it is clear that FICA is an "income" tax on "wages" paid for "employment", which is "service" performed within the Commonwealth of Puerto Rico, the Virgin Islands, Guam, and American Samoa; or outside of those places if by a citizen or resident thereof, and for the United States, a U.S.

possession government, or a company either owned by residents of the Commonwealth of Puerto Rico, the Virgin Islands, Guam, and American Samoa, or incorporated under their laws or those of the District of Columbia. (Bear in mind that *"within"* and *"resident of"* are terms *"used in a geographical sense";* 'citizenship' has geographical connotations as well.)

The taxes known as Federal Unemployment Taxes, or FUTA taxes, are similarly circumscribed:

> *Sec. 3301. - Rate of tax*
> *There is hereby imposed on every **employer (as defined in section 3306(a))** for each calendar year an excise tax, with respect to having individuals in his employ, equal to -* [rate of tax]
> *Sec. 3306. - Definitions*
> *(a) **Employer***
> *For purposes of this chapter -*
> *(1) In general*
> *The term "employer" means, with respect to any calendar year, any person who -*
> *(A)*
> *during any calendar quarter in the calendar year or the preceding calendar year paid **wages** of $1,500 or more, or*
> *(B)*
> *On each of some 20 during the calendar year or during the preceding calendar year, each day being in a different calendar week, **employed at least one individual in employment** for some portion of the day.*
> *(b) **Wages***
> *For purposes of this chapter, the term "wages" means all **remuneration for employment**, including the cash value of all remuneration (including benefits) paid in any medium other than cash;*

> *(c)* ***Employment***
> *For purposes of this chapter, the term "employment" means any* ***service*** *performed prior to 1955, which was employment for purposes of subchapter C of chapter 9 of the Internal Revenue Code of 1939 under the law applicable to the period in which such service was performed, and*
> *(A)*
> ***any service, of whatever nature, performed after 1954*** *by an employee for the person employing him, irrespective of the citizenship or residence of either,*
> *(i)*
> ***within the United States****, or*
> *...*

The definitions go on to duplicate-- for all practical purposes-- those previously enjoyed in our exploration of section 3121.

We must all be appreciative of the drafter's weakness of craft in this portion of the code. *"...employed at least one individual in employment...".* This construction is revealingly clumsy and ridiculous. It was critical to work the term *"employment"* into this portion of the statute, because it is by means of the definition of that term, confining affected parties to "service"-related government workers and those of U.S. possession-based companies, that the law remains Constitutional. It could not simply say, *"...employed at least one individual for some portion of the day."* as it would if the tax legally applied to every worker or business.

By the way, despite decades of relentless and shameless lies to the contrary by anyone with a stake in the deception unlikely to be sued over them, all of these Social Security taxes are nothing but "income" taxes like any other-- they have no relationship to any "trust accounts". It's possible that "trust accounts" may have been part of an original accounting structure. Certainly, rhetoric to that effect was deployed in the introduction of the scheme, serving as a legal and political fig-leaf behind which it obscured itself long enough for the formation of a cadre of constituents sure to defend the program at the ballot box. (The initial ranks of that cadre paid virtually nothing in FICA taxes themselves while receiving full benefits-- for instance, the very first beneficiary, Ida May Fuller, paid a total of only $24.75 in taxes but collected $22,888.92 in benefits.) But even if "trust accounts" were really intended to be a formal part of the scheme, they were dropped early.

Here is the portion of "Subtitle C- Employment Taxes" in which the true disposition of these taxes is revealed:

> *Sec. 3501. - Collection and payment of taxes*
> *(a) General rule*
> *The taxes imposed by this subtitle shall be collected by the Secretary and shall be paid into the Treasury of the United States as internal-revenue collections.*

This language was added to the code after an appellate court ruled, in a suit brought by a stockholder trying to stop a railroad from paying the tax, that no group (current workers) could be taxed to provide benefits (trust account financing) to any other group (retirees). In the subsequent Supreme Court hearing, in which that issue and a challenge of the program's taxes as direct yet unapportioned were considered, the government declined to defend the "trust account" concept. Instead, it argued that the "accounts" were a fiction; and pointed out that the taxes were excises. (No effort was made to suggest that the 'direct tax' challenge was moot due to the Sixteenth Amendment-- the government knew better.) The court agreed that the act only involved indirect taxes, and thus abided by the Constitution's requirements in that respect; but made clear that it felt the same as the lower court about the "trust account" thing. So, Congress quietly added section 3501 to the law. The marketing of the scheme as an insurance program remained the same, though, and hasn't changed since.

Crafting A Trade Or Business Plan: A Guide For The Self-Employed

ᵙᴓᴓᵙ

The way in which the Internal Revenue Code acknowledges the limited application of its provisions regarding the 'self-employed'-- by which is generally meant, as far as the code is concerned, patronage beneficiaries performing work for, and being paid by, the federal government-- is of the same misleading and obfuscating character as that relating to "employees". Only the persistent legal spelunker will delve deeply enough to learn that, contrary to superficial appearances, the related portions of the code have nothing to do with or say about private-sector entrepreneurs.

Here is the statutory language concerning "self-employment income", upon which the code imposes a "self-employment tax":

> *Sec. 1401. - Rate of tax*
> *(a) Old-age, survivors, and disability insurance*
> *In addition to other taxes, there shall be imposed for each taxable year, on the* ***self-employment income*** *of every individual, a tax equal to the following percent of the amount of the* ***self-employment income*** *for such taxable year:...*

Sec. 1402. - Definitions
(a) Net earnings from self-employment
*The term "**net earnings from self-employment**" means the gross income derived by an individual from any **trade or business** carried on by such individual, less the deductions allowed by this subtitle which are attributable to such **trade or business**,...*
*(b) **Self-employment income***
*The term "**self-employment income**" means the **net earnings from self-employment** derived by an individual...*

So far, one might be forgiven for imagining that anyone plying a trade, or maintaining a business, is subject to taxation of their "net" receipts, which is to say, those earnings from their work left over after a certain list of government-approved expenses (which do not include-- among much else-- food, clothing, shelter, heat, entertainment, savings, etc.) have been accounted for. But, when we indulge our suspicious nature and look further, we find:

Sec. 7701. - Definitions
(a) When used in this title, where not otherwise distinctly expressed or manifestly incompatible with the intent thereof -
*(26) **Trade or business***
*The term "**trade or business" includes the performance of the functions of a public office**.*

(There is a narrower version of this definition at 1402(c), but its distinctions are immaterial. See the appendix for more on this.)

The term *"trade or business"* is obviously the key definitional lynch-pin in this area of the code, just as are those of *"wages"* and *"employment"* in the withholding and FICA-FUTA sections. Look at the basic statutory obligation upon clients to distribute a '1099', notice of "income" paid, with which anyone who works for himself or herself is so well acquainted:

> *Sec. 6041 - Information at source*
> *(a) Payments of $600 or more*
> *All persons engaged in a **trade or business** and making payment in the course of such **trade or business** to another person, of rent, salaries, wages, premiums, annuities, compensations, remunerations, emoluments, or other fixed or determinable **gains, profits, and income** ... ...of $600 or more...shall render a true and accurate return...*

and:

> *Sec. 6041A. - Returns regarding payments of remuneration for services and direct sales*
> *(a) Returns regarding remuneration for services*
> *If -*
> *(1)*
> *any service-recipient engaged in a **trade or business** pays in the course of such **trade or business** during any calendar year remuneration to any person for services performed by such person, and*
> *(2)*
> *The aggregate of such remuneration paid to such person during such calendar year is $600 or more, then the service-recipient shall make a return...*

The instructions accompanying the forms themselves are even more explicit:

> ***Trade or business reporting only.*** *Report on Form 1099-MISC **only** when payments are made in the course of your **trade or business**.*

It should hardly need pointing out by now that there is no reasonable explanation for the particular use of the term *"trade or business"* in the language above except to invoke the custom, narrow legal definition in 7701(a)(26)-- if these sections were able to embrace anyone not involved in *"the performance of the functions of a public office"* they would simply say *"any person making a payment of other than personal funds amounting to $600* [as of this writing] *or more shall..."*. That is, of course, exactly how the beneficiaries of the scheme hope that this language will be misunderstood.

Frankly, though it demands a bit more mental energy than it may be worth (as the statute says what it means and means what it says), one might even wonder why this easily misunderstood language of the information reporting requirements is confined to payments by a business. Is there any reasonable justification for not requiring a homeowner paying Joe the plumber $1500 to outfit the new addition on the house to file a 1099 when the owner of Sam's Bar & Grill, paying Joe the plumber $1500 to outfit the new addition on the bar, must? It's not as though it would be an intolerable paperwork burden. Joe could even be required to bring the forms out with him; or the homeowner could be given them when getting the building permit for what is, after all, for most people a rare event. (The impropriety of the requirement for building permits is an evil not on the agenda for this book, wait for the sequel).

After all, lacking such a mechanism, we have to presume a ferocious amount of revenue is changing hands unreported-- it hardly seems fair that every tradesman should be afforded such opportunities for skating under the taxman's radar. Of course, creating the misunderstanding needed to plug this particular gap would mean giving up the *"trade or business"* connection...

But this is all just idle diversion. Both section 6041 and section 6041A depend on the *"trade or business"* language. What's more, section 6041 clearly instructs us that it only concerns payments of *"gains, profits, and income"*, and we know that the only way a payor could know that such is the character of a payment would be if that payor is a federal governmental unit paying a counterpart. There's a reason that it doesn't say, *"making payment in the course of such trade or business to another person of **money** totaling $600 or more".*

6041A has a slightly different clarifying element additional to the *"trade or business"* language, buried inside. Look again at paragraph (a)(1):

> *(1)*
> *any service-recipient engaged in a **trade or business** pays in the course of such **trade or business** during any calendar year remuneration to any **person** for services performed by such **person**, and...*

When we delve a little further into the smelly bowels of the section, 337 words later we find the following:

> *(d) Applications to governmental units*
> *(1) Treated as persons*
> *The term "person" includes any governmental unit (and any agency or instrumentality thereof).*

*****

Consistent with the general pattern throughout the code, the language which might mislead many who are self-employed into imagining an obligation to create and submit a return about themselves where one does not really exist deploys concealed custom definitions:

> *Sec. 6017. - Self-employment tax returns*
> *Every individual (other than a nonresident alien individual) having **net earnings from self-employment** of $400 or more for the taxable year shall make a return with respect to the self-employment tax imposed by chapter 2.*

It could say,

> *"Every self-employed individual (other than a nonresident alien individual) having earnings after*

deductions of $400 or more for the taxable year shall...."

But then the key term in this area of the law-- *"trade or business"*-- would not be incorporated, and the requirement would be unlawful. This section, like section 1401 by which a tax appears to be laid on the self-employed, relies on the definition of *"net earnings from self-employment"* found in section 1402 despite being, at an educated guess, 1,000,000 or so words away from it. Remember from the beginning of this section that the tax is imposed on the *"self-employment income"*... which term is later (in a whole different section of the law) defined as actually being the *"net earnings from self-employment"*... which term had been custom-defined itself *earlier* in the section as the *"gross income derived by an individual from any trade or business"*... which term is itself custom-defined a few hundred thousand words later in the code...

Are we having fun yet?

Always ask yourself, "Why is it written like this? Is it written like this because it means what its beneficiaries want me to believe that it means, or is it written like this because it *doesn't* mean what its beneficiaries want me to believe that it means?"

It seems pretty clear that unless one's works involves the performance of the functions of a public office one has no *"net earnings from self-employment"* and need file no return regarding the proceeds of self-employment; and no private-sector person or company should ever issue a 1099 MISC.

*****

From this point forward, we are mostly going to examine the nuts and bolts of the "income" tax scheme-- how it is implemented and administered. It is worthwhile, I think, to summarize the key points that we have covered so far regarding the nature of the tax:

The Constitution prohibits capitations and other direct taxes without apportionment. The Supreme Court has declared the meaning of "income" to be fixed and confined to objects proper to an excise. Objects proper to an "income" excise are privileges-- which is to say, activities not of common right-- and even then only to the extent that such activities are profitable and properly fall under the taxing authority's jurisdiction.

Consequently, the *only* lawful objects of the "income" tax are activities for which one is paid by the federal government or a federal agency or instrumentality; activities effectively connected with the performance of the functions of a public office; activities as a federal, federal instrumentality, or federally chartered "State" worker; or activities as a paid officer of a federal corporation, such as those on this not necessarily comprehensive list:

- *the Central Bank for Cooperatives*;
- *the Federal Deposit Insurance Corporation*;
- *the Federal Home Loan Banks*;
- *the Federal Intermediate Credit Banks*;
- *the Federal Land Banks*;
- *the Regional Banks for Cooperatives*;
- *the Rural Telephone Bank*;
- *the Financing Corporation*;
- *the Resolution Trust Corporation*;
- *the Resolution Funding Corporation*;
- *the Commodity Credit Corporation*;
- *the Community Development Financial Institutions Fund*;
- *the Export-Import Bank of the United States*;
- *the Federal Crop Insurance Corp.*;
- *Federal Prison Industries, Inc.*;
- *the Corp. for National and Community Service*;

- *the Government National Mortgage Association*;
- *the Overseas Private Investment Corporation*;
- *the Pennsylvania Avenue Development Corp.*;
- *the Pension Benefit Guaranty Corp.*;
- *the Saint Lawrence Seaway Development Corp.*;
- *the Tennessee Valley Authority*; the *Panama Canal Commission*;

and

- *the Alternative Agricultural Research and Commercialization Corp.*

As we have learned, it is only upon these activities that Congress has actually laid the tax.

We have also seen that the amount of taxable activity engaged in is measured by the receipts it produces, which are themselves misleadingly referred to as "income", and are treated, for all practical purposes, as the thing being taxed. (The convention is meaningless as far as how much tax is paid, but it contributes to the scheme by producing the appearance that the law lays a tax on the receipt of money). Thus, another way of summarizing what is taxed would be:

> *Remuneration or benefits (either immediate or deferred) paid by the federal government, its agencies, instrumentalities and "State" governments;*

and,

> *The proceeds of, and from, federal corporations and instrumentalities (such as those listed above, as well as national banks, railroads, etc.); and the proceeds of, and from, the conduct of a "trade or business".*

The total amount of "income" measured, by the way, is characterized as "gross income" within the revenue statutes. This is then refined down to nominal profitability-- the element transforming "gross income" into "taxable income" (called "net income" until 1954)-- by the application of available deductions, exemptions, and so forth.

Interlude

"There are two distinct classes of men...those who pay taxes and those who receive and live upon taxes." - Thomas Paine

I am confident there are those reading this book who still, even at this point, harbor lingering doubts as to the truth of the limited reach of the "income" tax revealed here. This is understandable and readily forgiven, as the habits of a lifetime are not quickly and easily overcome-- especially habits of thought. Habits of thought that are reinforced day-in and day-out by dedicated beneficiaries of the status quo are particularly persistent. Such doubts will express themselves as one or another version of the, *"How can this be true when I hear so much to the contrary, and the law appears to be enforced in defiance of what you say?"*

I must point out to such doubters that they are obliged by self-honesty to find themselves on the horns of a dilemma. In light of the Supreme Court's clear and repeated expressions regarding the untaxable nature of private activities, the virtually moot effect of the 16th Amendment, and the restricted meaning of the term "income"-- along with the sufficiently clear written letter of the law-- there are only a couple of possible truths to compete with that presented here.

One, of course, is that you personally are simply incapable of understanding the law-- either because it is possessed of a mystical character incomprehensible to normal persons, or because there is something wrong with you. As to the latter, I will assure you that if you have made it to this point in this book, you are perfectly OK, at least insofar as your intellectual and academic capacities are concerned.

As to the former, we have already discussed the nature of proper law. If you have disagreed with me on that subject, and are content that the law should be a mysterious, self-contradictory thing accessible only through the scryings of a priestly class, go from us now, for no words or evidence will sway you from surrender to the blandishments and ambitions of the corrupt and powerful. Their lust is your law and you will not raise your bowed head.

Another possibility is that I am just "cherry-picking", culling out only such rulings, statutes and other evidence from the whole body available as support my contentions. Well, even if this were true, the very existence of such evidence to be "cherry-picked" would render any to the contrary that might exist to be at least ambiguous, if not outright overborne, and thus, in either case, void. As the Supreme Court has instructed us in Connally v. General Const. Co., 269 U.S. 385 (1926):

> *"...a statute which either forbids or requires the doing of an act in terms so vague that men of common intelligence must necessarily guess at its meaning and differ as to its application violates the first essential of due process of law."*

At bottom, that protest, which presumes that there is somewhere a contradictory body of evidence in support of the current regime, is a hollow attempt to reverse the burden of proof, compelling the questions of why is MY body of evidence extant, and where is the other? Ah, yes... it is in the hands of the priests, and not to be looked upon by mere laymen! Really, lacking such contradictory evidence in hand, and faced with what is, this is merely a version of "mysterious law".

What is left is that what I say about the law is true, and the apparent contradiction with the ways things are is the consequence of a conspiracy in defiance of that truth. Such a conspiracy might be imagined as one in which judges, prosecutors, bureaucrats, politicians and professionals-- knowing the truth-- simply act in blithe and blatant disregard of the law as written and ruled upon. They want the money and don't give a damn what the law says, and somehow nobody else knows or cares. This is the "Invasion of the Body Snatchers" scenario. If it's true, you should be reading this in a bunker in the hills.

Of course, if such a wide-spread, deeply rooted *conscious* conspiracy existed there would be plenty of evidence to support the conspirators-- they could make their own, after all-- and I would have none. Then I would be back to arguing against the propriety of the law, rather than having little more to do than to point out what it actually says. The fact is, the "Body Snatchers" thing is an oversimplification of the much murkier and, in its way, more sordid reality. (At least the "Body Snatchers" thing would amount to a relatively straightforward conquest of tax-payers by tax-consumers, without necessarily generating a corrupting influence extending much beyond the area of taxes themselves. More about that later in 'Why It Matters').

There's a wonderful old fable called "The Emperor's New Clothes" in which a pair of scoundrels con money from a foolish sovereign by claiming the ability to spin clothes from pure gold. The Emperor, eager to have what he should have known was impossible, gives them his gold and a room in which to work, but prudently attempts to supervise them through the eyes of various members of his court, whom he dispatches at intervals to observe and report on the progress of the work. However, the two conmen, through sheer audacity and an exploitation of the human psychology, oblige each such officer to conclude, or at least presume, that the imaginary clothes which the pair claim to be sewing (while really just engaging in pantomime) are visible to every one but himself.

The scheme is sublime. An expansive and eloquent sincerity in presenting the non-existent work for inspection is coupled with the assertion that only those unfit for high station could fail to see the wonderful new raiment-- precluding those who might be inclined to believe their own eyes from voicing, or even seriously entertaining, their doubts. Quite the contrary, in fact: each victim of the scam is seduced into personal participation, vociferously praising the magnificence of the work, so as to not be thought unfit, and encouraging their fellows to do the same while marginalizing the unenthusiastic. The cunning process instantly created a community of interest in the perpetuation-- even the elaboration-- of the illusion. So, the fantasy is spun and continues, not only unchallenged but ever-fed, until the Emperor himself, having been told over and over by all of his subordinates what wonderful work the conmen are doing (and, no less than any other, unwilling to raise doubts regarding his own fitness for office), effusively praises the invisible garments with which he is at last fitted, and marches naked into the public square to show off his new finery. The thieves sneak away with all the gold, which they have, of course, simply pocketed.

I hope that everyone shares this most educational tale with their children. This fable speaks to much of human behavior and particularly the foibles of institutionalized power, but to nothing more closely and instructively today than to the corruption of the rule of law in the United States.

Many lessons can be drawn from "the Emperor's New Clothes"-- among them, never send a subordinate to do a sovereign's work; which is to say, don't rely on a servant to report on the other servant's performance. More to the immediate point, this parable teaches us that a con devised so as to invoke the interests of those who might expose it stands a good chance of remaining unchallenged. Privilege will defend itself, with utter nonsense if necessary; and a community of interest once created will become a political force protective of that interest-- a conspiracy without an explicit plot, but nonetheless advancing a common agenda. The "income" tax scheme is a con benefiting from, and relying upon, all of these weaknesses and flaws of human nature and liberal political systems.

It is not necessary to identify the scoundrels who first conceived of (or quietly enabled) the mass deception in order to recognize the venal interests perfectly willing to exploit and expand it, once established. These interests-- the spenders of the money brought in by the scheme, the professional industries administering and defending against it, every lazy or callow judge who couldn't be troubled to actually read the law, and the bureaucratic establishment employed by it-- all benefit from the con, and do indeed form a conspiracy, but not a hard, cold and calculated conspiracy. Rather, it is a soft and loose conspiracy-- after the fashion of a parasitic infestation. Each individual parasite isn't necessarily aware of the activities of its fellows, but each in undirected concert contributes to the destruction of the host.

It is a conspiracy of sloth, and ignorance, and plunder, and fear. And a good share of corruption and lies, of course. Some of those mentioned above at least suspect the truth; a few of them know.

A different category of contributors to the casual conspiracy are the direct beneficiaries of the scheme-- those actually being handed the money outright, rather than getting their piece of the action dressed up as pay or fees-for-service related to the administration of the tax. They and their intellectual camp-followers generate and disseminate a massive body of historical, social and economic bilge in order to keep the host lying quietly for the feeding.

This sort of nonsense takes many forms. One example is the patently absurd but relentlessly promoted myth that, as regards taxes, a great social contract is in play in which one citizen pays for programs of limited or zero value to themselves, but desired and enjoyed by another in order to ensure that that 'other' will cooperatively reciprocate in their turn. We are assured by the promoters of this notion that such a system of give-and-take is fundamental to our form of government and/or basic practical politics and social justice.

The cold, hard truth, however, is that most-- if not all-- of those of us who pay the freight will never receive a corresponding benefit unless it is in our plans to go on the dole or become a bureaucrat or similar tax parasite, joining the ranks of the net-tax-beneficiaries. Even if we do one of those things our bills will not then be paid by the trough-snufflers,... we'll just add another mouth to the burden of our former fellows in the net-tax-paying herd. The only patina of reciprocity to be wrung from that would be that in abiding our own fleecing earlier we help perpetuate the system which we later exploit for our own benefit.

Another soporific delusion offered for our consumption is that our highly qualified leaders and government workers strive diligently to identify necessary and proper objects upon which to expend the wealth extracted from us for the benefit of the nation as a whole. (Conveniently, once the reciprocity myth mentioned above has been embraced, the national necessity one is proof against almost any casual assault-- any given program or expenditure may not make sense or seem beneficial to *you*, but doubtless does to one of those '*others*'-- the nature and interests of whom need never be unambiguously identified).

The cold, hard truth is that the political class and its government employee clients and co-conspirators routinely and deliberately promote narrow-interest programs because each one means another little piece of pie (administrative overhead) with which comfortable jobs for the bureaucrats are secured, along with dedicated political support from the beneficiaries by which *very* comfortable jobs and celebrity for the politicians are secured. The cold, hard truth is that those of us who pay the taxes are dupes. We are naifs. We are *marks*.

"Find out just what any people will quietly submit to and you have the exact measure of the injustice and wrong which will be imposed on them."
-Frederick Douglass

A third vein of mythology being worked to keep the cattle quiet is that if we really *were* being victimized by a fraudulent system for the benefit of others, we would be stripped to our underwear and left penniless-- lucky to escape with our lives. Since this is not so, what is done must be legitimate, however incomprehensible or counter-intuitive it may be. This clever, subtextual argument is reliant upon a widespread ignorance of history (providing one of many self-interested reasons government schools de-emphasize history so purposefully) and is nurtured by an ever-more-juvenile news and entertainment industry.

The fact is, conquest and subjugation by parasites from within a democratic framework doesn't work the same as an assault by external predators. However ultimately fatal an unchecked infestation of net-tax-beneficiaries is to a polity, parasites, being small and incapable, do not seek to kill their hosts-- they just mean to make an easy living off of them. Read this paragraph from a U.S. Postal Service workers website, Postalvoice.com:

> *By the time our average federal employee reaches 30 years of service in 2012, he will be 59 years old, his annual salary will be $90,721 and his high three average salary will be $82,880. He will be entitled to $46,620 annual retirement annuity without the survivor benefit. If he elects a full survivor benefit, then his annual annuity will be $42,228 (annual cost of the survivor benefit is $4,392) and his survivor would receive $25,641 annually if he died in 2012.*
>
> ***At retirement, he takes a loss of more than 50% on annual income***

(The emphasis in the above complaint-- yes, it's a complaint-- is in the original).

These cited statistics-- which are for the year 2000, by the way-- refer to the circumstances of your letter carrier, and the IRS agent who audits your tax return, among others. Several million others.

On the other hand, the 2000 median income for all ages in the United States overall, according to the U.S. Census Bureau's Sept., 2001 report "Money Income In The United States: 2000" was $42,148, less than the grumbled-at *retirement pay* of your letter-carrier. Think about that. The people who extract your earnings from you and your neighbors-- for the common good, of course-- pay themselves and their colleagues twice as much of those earnings as you nominally receive (before the taxes are taken from you). I guess that's why such people claim with a straight face that taxes aren't anything to make a fuss about-- even after the bite they're still living pretty large. (At least the arrangement should act as a natural check on the total number of federal employees that can be fastened upon the country-- even if the wealth producers were left with nothing for themselves, they could not maintain the bureaucracy in the style to which they have become accustomed at more than a one-out-of-three bureaucrat-to-productive-citizen ratio.)

Let's face it. Someone getting paid $90,000 in tax money-- extracted by force or fraud-- for a level of effort and talent that would get $42,000 in the free market (at most-- these aren't brain-surgeon level skills being considered here) is no less a villain because they don't, or can't yet, escalate their predations to even higher levels. Similarly, a "professional" making an easy living cadging fees from anxious, traumatized, victims of a fraudulently administered tax scheme is no less a villain for contenting himself with whatever charges the market will bear for his "protective services". (Particularly not while lobbying for more complexity and increased vigor in the tax system, in order to help the market bear more. Consider the declaration by Gerald Padwe, representing the American Institute of Certified Public Accountants in a March 8th 2002 interview with National Public Radio, that the IRS should conduct more audits. He alleged that this is necessary in order to support Americans' "faith in the system". Personally, I can't see why such faith has any particular interest for members of the AICPA. It is no more their natural concern than is your attitude toward the administration of the municipal water system to the plumber you hire to fix the pipes. More audits DO result in more business for CPA's, though; and, of course, in light of the truth about the income tax, the interest of the profession in nurturing a faith-based acceptance of the status-quo is manifest).

Likewise, someone living at the expense of their neighbor through a public subsidy, and especially one for which they themselves voted, is no less a villain for letting co-conspirators do the hands-on stealing amid nonsense about "Social Contracts" or "Civic Responsibilities". Fatuous declarations by the likes of Oliver Wendell Holmes Jr.

notwithstanding, taxes are not "the price we pay for civilization". Nazi Germany had taxes, and plenty of them; as has had every other barbaric regime throughout history. The inconvenience attendant upon scrupulous respect for the rights of our neighbor, including his right to his property and the fruits of his labor, is the price we pay for civilization.

It may well be true that a certain amount of taxation is practically unavoidable. (It may well not be true either-- but I am not seeking to make that case in this book). However, we are provided with Constitutional forms for the practice that are not only adequate to any legitimate national need, but are at the same time protective of the liberty which is, after all, the only reason for which the state and its taxing powers have been instituted.

We have already discussed direct taxes under the Constitution, and why the Founders opposed them in principle and instituted hobbling safeguards by which to ensure against abuse. Alexander Hamilton, in Federalist #21, provides a useful little summary of the principles of the alternative provided, indirect taxes, for which only the rule of uniformity is necessary:

> *"Imposts, excises, and, in general, all duties upon articles of consumption, may be compared to a fluid, which will, in time, find its level with the means of paying them. The amount to be contributed by each citizen will in a degree be at his own option, and can be regulated by an attention to his resources. The rich may be extravagant, the poor can be frugal; and private oppression may always be avoided by a judicious selection of objects proper for such impositions. If inequalities should arise in some States from duties on particular objects, these will, in all probability, be counterbalanced by proportional inequalities in other States, from the duties on other objects. In the course of time and things, an equilibrium, as far as it is*

attainable in so complicated a subject, will be established everywhere. Or, if inequalities should still exist, they would neither be so great in their degree, so uniform in their operation, nor so odious in their appearance, as those which would necessarily spring from quotas, upon any scale that can possibly be devised.

It is a signal advantage of taxes on articles of consumption, that they contain in their own nature a security against excess. They prescribe their own limit; which cannot be exceeded without defeating the end proposed, that is, an extension of the revenue. When applied to this object, the saying is as just as it is witty, that, "in political arithmetic, two and two do not always make four".

If duties are too high, they lessen the consumption; the collection is eluded; and the product to the treasury is not so great as when they are confined within proper and moderate bounds. This forms a complete barrier against any material oppression of the citizens by taxes of this class, and is itself a natural limitation of the power of imposing them."

The uniformity rule, though previously argued as meaning "If the sale of a widget carries a $10 tax in Idaho, then it must also carry a $10 tax in Vermont", is better understood today. Modern scholarship-- and simple clear-headedness-- is revealing that the "uniformity" requirement is intended to ensure that the distribution of taxes, region by region, is as uniform as it could be made. In other words, it is to ensure that the federal government cannot impose a tax in connection with an item used only, or far more commonly, in any particular region which would thus bear a disproportionate share of the burden of maintaining the national government. It is by the means of this requirement that the Founders seek to enforce

Hamilton's "equilibrium". (The requirement of equal treatment under the law sees to the other kind of uniformity).

Sadly, the virtue or purpose of this principle, which is intended for application to tariffs as well as internal indirect taxes, was disregarded during the mid 19th century. The Northern States, which, being more populous, dominated Congress, saw to the enactment of tariffs protective of their well-established and politically active manufacturing interests. Southern States, whose economies were based on exports and who were importers of the tariff-affected goods became wildly disproportionate net-tax-paying States compared to the North. By 1858, the South was paying 87% of the total tariff. This situation strongly influenced the decision by the South to secede, resulting in the War Between the States.

*****

In an earlier part of our history, such as that in which "The Emperor's New Clothes" is set, the institutional villains of the time deployed the mythology of "the divine right of kings" (along with state-sponsored terrorism against resistors) to keep their victims passive or confused and disorganized. Such myths supplemented and gradually replaced the massive violence of the original conquest by arms as the means of the collection from the subject population of tribute-- the original word for "taxes". This transformational process was a consequence of the conquerors and the subject population's blending together, with the outright master-slave relationship being softened somewhat by the development of traditions, ritual, etc. Now we have the situation in reverse, in which a tribute-claiming (or, at least, consuming) class is forming and detaching itself from the larger population, with barely a peep from citizens who wouldn't hesitate to throw a fit if the grocer tried to overcharge them by a nickel.

It may yet be a bit early to start teaching your children how to curtsey and bow; but unless wealth-producers and those who love liberty assert themselves, in due course they'll need such skills. As it stands, when you hand your tax return to the clerk at the post office this year, show some respect. After all, until things change, he's one of the people you work for.

"If ye love wealth greater than liberty, the tranquility of servitude greater than the animating contest for freedom, go home from us in peace. We seek not your counsel, nor your arms. Crouch down and lick the hand that feeds you. May your chains set lightly upon you; and may posterity forget that ye were our countrymen". -Samuel Adams

Part Two
(The Nature Of The Scheme)

"Only mustard isn't a bird," Alice remarked.
"Right, as usual," said the Duchess: "what a clear way you have of putting things!"
"It's a mineral, I think," said Alice.
"Of course it is," said the Duchess, who seemed ready to agree to everything that Alice said: "there's a large mustard mine near here. And the moral of that is-- 'The more there is of mine, the less there is of yours.'"
"Oh, I know!" exclaimed Alice, who had not attended to this last remark. "It's a vegetable. It doesn't look like one, but it is."
"I quite agree with you," said the Duchess; "and the moral of that is-- 'Be what you would seem to be'-- or, if you'd like to put it more simply-- 'Never imagine yourself not to be otherwise than what it might appear to others that what you were or might have been was not otherwise than what you had been would have appeared to them to be otherwise.'"
"I think I should understand that better," Alice said very politely, "if I had it written down: but I can't quite follow it as you say it."
"That's nothing to what I could say if I chose," the Duchess replied in a pleased tone.

"W" Is For Weapon

ഇരു

The revenue laws are a code or system in regulation of tax assessment and collection. They relate to taxpayers, and not to nontaxpayers. The latter are without their scope. No procedure is prescribed for nontaxpayers, and no attempt is made to annul any of their rights and remedies in due course of law. With them Congress does not assume to deal, and they are neither of the subject nor of the object of the revenue laws." United States Court of Claims, Economy Plumbing and Heating v. United States, 470 F.2d 585, at 589 (1972)

"*The IRS's primary task is to collect taxes under a voluntary compliance system*"—Jerome Kurtz, IRS Commissioner.

"*Our tax system is based on individual self-assessment and voluntary compliance.*"—Mortimer Caplin, IRS Commissioner.

"*Each year American taxpayers voluntarily file their tax returns...*"—Johnnie Walters, IRS Commissioner.

"*The income tax system is based upon voluntary compliance, not distraint*", United States Supreme Court, Flora v. United States, 362 US 145.

Despite the actual statutory construction of the "income" tax law, scrupulously Constitutional and compliant with the various rulings of the Supreme Court, it is routinely applied to untaxable activities/receipts in defiance of those legal requirements-- at enormous cost to countless individuals and to society itself. This is accomplished by means of deception, corruption and intimidation. We have looked at several of the chief building blocks on which the scheme rests in the "employment tax" and "self-employment" sections of the code; now we will look at the instruments by which their ill effects are brought to bear.

The scheme is complex and artful. Because of the limitations of the federal taxing power, the government must somehow create a body of evidence from which to allege that *untaxable* activities are actually *taxable* activities before it can assert a claim of authority, or legal interest.

Being unable to declare private-sector, unprivileged activities to be subject to the tax, or to-- itself-- declare that a private-sector individual engaged in taxable activities, the government instead attempts to cause private-sector individuals to legally declare-- for themselves-- that payments with which they are associated involved taxable activities.

This is accomplished by inducing such persons to execute affidavits of various kinds which support presumptions that their payments or receipts occurred as federal (or federally-subordinate-- i.e., territory or possession) government workers; in connection with the performance of a federal (or federally subordinate) public office; or as a profitable result of investment or other participation in federal, federally-connected or federally-controlled corporations, partnerships and other such entities. These affidavits then serve as the desired evidence.

Although in this respect the scheme is constructively fraudulent, it is implemented with careful attention to not crossing the line beyond which explicit criminal culpability of the government and its actors arises. In fact, where the success of the scheme relies on actually engaging in legally liable behavior, it is mostly private-sector business owners who are tricked into bearing the burden of the risk. At the same time, though the victims whose wealth is the target of the flim-flam are themselves tricked into enabling the processes brought to bear against them, the law as written imposes no requirement to do so. This is what is meant by "voluntary compliance" with the income tax-- citizens under no obligation to do so voluntarily participate in, or leave unchallenged, the processes by which their untaxable receipts are transformed into taxable benefits of privilege.

"Let me point this out now. Your income tax is 100 percent voluntary tax, and your liquor tax is 100 percent enforced tax. Now the situation is as different as day and night. Consequently, your same rules just will not apply." Testimony of Dwight E. Avis, Head of the Alcohol and Tobacco Tax Division of the Bureau of Internal Revenue, before the House Ways and Means Committee on Restructuring the IRS (83rd Congress, 1953).

The careful and deliberate use of the phrase "voluntary compliance" by the IRS is instructive. It is intended, as is so much else associated with the modern administration of the "income" tax, to confuse and mislead-- in this case by suggesting that we choose to comply with a legal obligation without too much fuss, or the like. However, "voluntary compliance" is not a mystical religious term embracing two contradictory concepts. It means that individuals comply as a matter of choice because they cannot be forced to do so... as one complies with a request. Such language would not be used under any circumstances were compliance actually required. The draft was never described as relying upon "voluntary compliance" howevermuch 18 year-olds were encouraged to take it upon themselves to register on their own without being thrown in prison first.

Under the mystical self-contradictory reading of the phrase which the government would prefer that we accept and not examine too closely, every law in the country could be described as relying upon voluntary compliance. They are not so described, because they are not so reliant. The assignment of taxable status to otherwise untaxable revenue-productive activities, self-assessment of the resulting tax, and the filing of a related income tax return by private-sector individuals are so described because they *are* voluntary. Voluntary compliance can only respond to a request or as a choice. It cannot and does not respond to a requirement.

"The word `voluntary', which connotes an agreement, implies willingness, volition, and intent. It suggests a freedom of choice and refers to the doing of something which a person is free to do or not to do, as he so decides.

...

In its legal aspect, and as commonly used in law, the word `voluntary' is defined as meaning gratuitous; without valuable consideration; acting, or done, of one's own free will without valuable consideration; acting, or done, without any present legal obligation to do the thing done." Corpus Juris Secundum (C.J.S. 92: 1029, 1030, 1031)

*****

The evidence by which a citizen's untaxable activities become presumptively taxable can take either of two forms--documents created and executed by others, (which are relatively easy to rebut) and documents created and executed by the victim (which are much harder to deal with, and therefore are much preferred by the government). The object of securing either kind of evidence is, once again, to establish that:

A. The target is a federal worker (by securing assertions or admissions of being an "employee", receiving "wages" and/or being engaged in a "trade or business") ; or
B. The target's funds come from the federal government; or
C. The target is a "United States person".

This last object-- establishing the status of an individual as a "United States person"-- supports several different elements of the federal tax structure (including some not involving the "income" tax, by the way). We will focus on this subject in detail in the next section. However, the term does appear in the content of *this* section as well. Thus, I'll go over its definition, which is found at 26 USC 7701(30), now:

> *(30) United States person*
>
> *The term "United States person" means -*
>
> *(A) a citizen or resident of the United States,*
> *(B) a domestic partnership,*
> *(C) a domestic corporation,*
> *(D) any estate (other than a foreign estate, within the meaning of paragraph (31)), and*
> *(E) any trust if -*
>
> *(i) a court within the United States is able to exercise primary supervision over the administration of the trust, and*
> *(ii) one or more United States persons have the authority to control all substantial decisions of the trust.);*

Note that all of the qualifying entities, including individual, natural persons, are so based upon their geographical circumstances. The definition of the term "United States" used in that of "United States person", also found in section 7701, is:

> *(9) United States*
>
> *The term "United States" when used in a geographical sense includes only the States and the District of Columbia.*

and that of "State", which is used in the definition of "United States", which is used in that of "United States person" and at which we looked previously in 'The Code Is Born', is:

> *(10) State*
>
> *The term "State" shall be construed to include the District of Columbia, where such construction is necessary to carry out provisions of this title.*

and, per section 7651 of the code, also includes:

> *...any possession of the United States in the same manner and to the same extent as if such possession were a State, and as if the term "United States" when used in a geographical sense included such possession.*

This one is tricky, I know. Remember, the reason there is a custom definition provided for something is because *it doesn't mean what you would otherwise think it means.*

As we proceed, we will examine how the most widely deployed of these instruments are commonly misused (and the effects thereof). Serendipitously, the nature of these chosen tools of fraud, and the vigor and subterfuge with which their use is promoted, will clearly confirm the specialized and limited lawful application of the "income" tax.

*****

A few words about the relationship between statutes and regulations is in order at this point, as we will necessarily be looking at both forms of the law as we proceed. First of all, it is important to understand that any regulation related to a statute is subordinate to the statute, just as all statutes are subordinate to the Constitution. Regulations cannot exceed the authority provided by the statute. Regulations *can* fall short of that authority, and therefore be to a citizen's advantage, because one need do no more than the regulations require to satisfy one's legal duty, even if the statute requires more. But one can never be required to do more or other than the statute provides. (A little advice to those obliged at any time to hire a "tax professional": I would not trust the work of any advisor or assistant who ever cites a regulation without including the statute to which it is subordinate-- and that does not mean the 'code' version of the statute, but the actual law itself).

> *"...we cannot but regard this Treasury Regulation as... ...an attempted addition to the statute of something which is not there. As such the regulation can furnish no sustenance to the statute."* (Citation omitted.) United States v. Calamaro, 354 U.S. 351 (1957)

One of the cleverest ploys of the scheme we are unraveling is the erratic and devious use of the regulatory implementation (or lack thereof) to technically confine the code within Constitutional limits, while concealing the consequent narrowness of its actual legal application. What I mean is that if a given statute lacks a critical term or reference making clear its restriction to a lawful subject of the tax, such as "trade or business" or "wages" etc., such a term or reference will be found in the regulations implementing that statute. In other cases, there will be no implementing regulations at all, despite language in the statute indicating that its application is dependent on *"such regulations as the Secretary may from time to time prescribe"*.

A statute can mislead the unwary while remaining lawful, if it imposes no requirement to act; or if it, or its associated regulations, contains clarifying elements. So, some statutes published in the code contain clarifying, limiting language themselves; others provide it within the regulations, and still others simply have no regulations and exist solely to provide the appearance of a claim of authority when, legally, none is actually being made.

We'll look at a few examples of this technique. First of all, consider sections 6041 and 6041A of the IRC which we examined in 'Crafting A Trade Or Business Plan...' in relation to requirements for the filing of 1099's. You will recall that they both remained Constitutional by incorporating the application-limiting terms *"trade or business"* and *"gains, profits and income"* (and that 6041A had its own little custom definition of *"person"*, as well) within the statutory language itself. Now look at the statutory language of another information return requirement:

> *Sec. 6045. - Returns of brokers*
>
> *(a) General rule*
>
> *Every person doing business as a broker shall, when required by the Secretary, make a return, in accordance with such regulations as the Secretary may prescribe, showing the name and address of each customer, with such details regarding gross proceeds and such other information as the Secretary may by forms or regulations require with respect to such business.*

Read alone, this looks like anybody who hangs out a shingle as a broker belongs to the Secretary. However, when we look at the implementing regulations we find:

> *§ 1.6045-1 Returns of information of brokers and barter exchanges.*
>
> *(a) Definitions. The following definitions apply for purposes of this section and § 1.6045-2:*
>
> *(1) The term broker means any person (other than a person who is required to report a transaction under section 6043), U.S. or foreign, that, in the ordinary*

course of a ***trade or business*** *during the calendar year, stands ready to effect sales to be made by others.*

So, the requirement is actually confined to those engaged in the conduct of a public office, just as in the case of 6041 and 6041A.

Not that anyone will be enthused to go through it, but here's a more complicated version of the same concealment of the application-limiting language in the regulations:

Sec. 6042. - Returns regarding payments of dividends and corporate earnings and profits
(a) Requirement of reporting
(1) In general
Every person -
(A)
who makes payments of dividends aggregating $10 or more to any other person during any calendar year,... shall make a return according to the forms or regulations prescribed by the Secretary, setting forth the aggregate amount of such payments and the name and address of the person to whom paid.

Reading that language alone, one would have to conclude that the government has decided to blatantly disregard the limitations on its power and is imposing involuntary servitude upon every private-sector accountant throughout the nation. (Or the world-- there is no limitation within this language). But if we look at the pertinent implementing regulations (with significant elements emphasized), we find:

§ 1.6042-2 Returns of information as to dividends paid.
(a) Requirement of reporting -- (1) In general. An information return on Form 1099 shall be made under section 6042(a) by --

> *(i) Every person who makes a payment of dividends* ***(as defined in § 1.6042-3)*** *to any other person during a calendar year.*

§ ***1.6042-3*** *Dividends subject to reporting.*
(b) ***Exceptions*** *-- (1) In general.* ***For purposes of §§ 1.6042-2 and 1.6042-4, the amounts described in paragraphs (b)(1)(i) through (vii) of this section are not dividends.***
(iv) *Distributions or payments from sources* ***outside the United States*** *(as determined under the provisions of part I, subchapter N, chapter 1 of the Code and the regulations under those provisions* [this reference is irrelevant but I decline demonstrating this here, as it would be wearisome to me and probably boring to you. Doubters are encouraged to examine the relevant section, 862, for themselves.]*)* ***paid outside the United States*** *by a* ***non-U.S. payor or a non-U.S. middleman. For a definition of non-U.S. payor and non-U.S. middleman, see § 1.6049-5(c)(5).***

(Before continuing, those still struggling with the *"includes"* thing might want to re-read 1.6042-3(b)(iv). If *"includes"* in the relevant definition is not read as limiting, and *"United States"* is thus read as meaning the 50 States as well as federal places and the possessions and territories (rather than what the words in its legal definition actually say), then what this regulation says is that an accountant in the Ukraine, for example, making a payment of dividends to someone outside the U.S. is excused from filing an information return with the IRS. Frankly, even without the generous dispensation of 1.6042-3(b)(iv), an accountant in the Ukraine would tell the IRS to stuff its reporting requirement even if he were sending dividends to a resident of Fairfax, Virginia or Dubuque, Iowa. What would be the point of this regulation? But reading *"includes"* and thus *"United States, when used in a geographical sense..."* as meaning what the words in their legal definitions actually say, this regulation simply and appropriately (and Constitutionally) confines the statute's effect to dividend-payors based in federal territory.)

Now to continue...

> ***§ 1.6049-5(c)(5) U.S. payor, U.S. middleman, non-U.S. payor, and non-U.S. middleman.*** *The terms payor and middleman have the meanings ascribed to them under § 1.6049-4(a). A non-U.S. payor or non-U.S. middleman means a payor or middleman other than a U.S. payor or U.S. middleman. The* ***term U.S. payor or U.S. middleman means*** *--*
>
> *(i) A person described in section 7701(a)(30) (including a foreign branch or office of such person);* [**a "U.S. person"**]
>
> *(ii) The* ***government of the United States*** *or the government of any State or political subdivision thereof (or any agency or instrumentality of any of the foregoing);*
>
> *(iii) A controlled foreign corporation within the meaning of section 957(a);* [**controlled by "United States" shareholders**]
>
> *(iv) A foreign partnership, if at any time during its tax year, one or more of its partners are* ***U.S. persons*** *(as defined in § 1.1441-1(c)(2)) who, in the aggregate hold more than 50 percent of the income or capital interest in the partnership or if, at any time during its tax year, it is engaged in the conduct of a* ***trade or business*** *in the United States;*
>
> *(v) A foreign person 50 percent or more of the gross income of which, from all sources for the three-year period ending with the close of its taxable year preceding the collection or payment (or such part of such period as the person has been in existence), was*

effectively connected with the conduct of ***trade or business*** *within the United States; or*
(vi) A ***U.S. branch*** *of a foreign bank or a foreign insurance company described in § 1.1441-1(b)(2)(iv).*

Whew! It's big, and it's brutal, and it does what it has to do.

Here's another use of the same handy, complex, application-limiting escape hatch:

Sec. 6050N. - Returns regarding payments of royalties
(a) Requirement of reporting
Every person -
(1)
who makes payments of royalties (or similar amounts) aggregating $10 or more to any other person during any calendar year,...
shall make a return according to the forms or regulations prescribed by the Secretary, setting forth the aggregate amount of such payments and the name and address of the person to whom paid.

and the pertinent regulations:

§ 1.6050N-1 Statements to recipients of royalties paid after December 31, 1986.
(a) Requirement. A person required to make an information return under section 6050N(a) must furnish a statement to each recipient whose name is required to be shown on the related information return for royalties paid.
(c) Exempted foreign-related items -- (1) In general. No return shall be required under paragraph (a) of this section for payments of the items described in paragraphs (c)(1)(i) through (iv) of this section.
(ii) Returns of information are not required for payments of royalties from sources outside the

> ***United States*** *(determined under Part I of subchapter N and the regulations under these provisions) made outside the United States by a non-U.S. payor or non-U.S. middleman. For a definition of non-U.S. payor or non-U.S. middleman, see § 1.6049-5(c)(5).*

...and so on.

One last example:

> *Sec. 6048. - Information with respect to certain foreign trusts*
>
> *(a) Notice of certain events*
>
> *(1) General rule*
>
> *On or before the 90th day (or such later day as the Secretary may prescribe) after any reportable event, the* ***responsible party shall provide written notice of such event to the Secretary in accordance with paragraph (2).***
>
> *(2) Contents of notice*
>
> ***The notice required by paragraph (1) shall contain such information as the Secretary may prescribe****, including -*
>
> *(A)*
>
> *the amount of money or other property (if any) transferred to the trust in connection with the reportable event, and*
>
> *(B)*
>
> *the identity of the trust and of each trustee and beneficiary (or class of beneficiaries) of the trust.*

and the associated regulations (in total):

Now on to the W's.

W-9's And Other Alien Notions

"Anyone entering into an arrangement with the government takes the risk of having accurately ascertained that he who purports to act for the government stays within the bounds of his authority, even though the agent himself may be unaware of the limitations upon his authority."
The United States Supreme Court, Federal Crop Ins. Corp. v. Merrill, 332 US 380-388 (1947)

Each of the code section examples (other than 6048) used in '"W" Is For Weapon' regarding regulatory sleight-of-hand, as well as the sections 6041 and 6041A at which we looked in 'Crafting a Trade Or Business Plan...' have a bearing on one of the evidentiary instruments used against private citizens to create a presumption of taxability. They are among the pretexts behind the Form W-9. The form, traditionally used primarily against contractors and investors, is now being more widely deployed. Due to a fairly new regulatory reform, one of the United States government instrumentalities with which the bulk of the general population necessarily interacts-- national banks-- are required to request the execution of the form from everyone opening an account. (*"National banks are instrumentalities of the federal government, created for a public purpose, and as such necessarily subject to the paramount authority of the United States."* Davis v. Elmira Savings, 161 U.S. 275 (1896))

In either case the purpose is ostensibly to secure a correct "taxpayer identification number" (with, in the case of the banks, no explanation provided as to the purpose of the request-- they make it even in association with non-interest paying accounts with which the tax system has and can have no lawful concern whatever). Cooperation by the target is sub-textually encouraged by the suggestion on the form that without its execution the requester will be obliged to withhold money from the requestee. We'll look at why the execution of this form is desired a bit later on. To begin with, let's examine the actual legal nature of the request.

Here is the certification language to which someone executing the form attests (from the 2003 form, and with some emphasis added; some is in the original):

> *Under penalties of perjury, I certify that:*
> *1. The number shown on this form is my correct* ***taxpayer identification number*** *(or I am waiting for a number to be issued to me), and*
> *2. I am not subject to backup withholding because: (a) I am exempt from backup withholding, or (b) I have not been notified by the Internal Revenue Service (IRS) that I am subject to backup withholding as a result of a failure to report all interest or dividends, or (c) the IRS has notified me that I am no longer subject to backup withholding, and*
> *3.* ***I am a U.S. person*** *(including a U.S. resident alien).*

Here is the stated purpose of the form:

Purpose of Form

*A person who **is required** to file an information return with the IRS, must obtain your correct taxpayer identification number (TIN) to report, for example, income paid to you, real estate transactions, mortgage interest you paid, acquisition or abandonment of secured property, cancellation of debt, or contributions you made to an IRA.*

***U.S. person**. Use Form W-9 **only if you are a U.S. person** (including a resident alien), to provide your correct TIN to the person requesting it (the requester) and, when applicable, to:*
1. Certify that the TIN you are giving is correct (or you are waiting for a number to be issued),
2. Certify that you are not subject to backup withholding,
or
3. Claim exemption from backup withholding if you are a U.S. exempt payee.

You will have noted that the completion of this form is to be requested by persons *required* to file a return about another person, per such sections as we have examined earlier. However, there is a specific statutory structure under which, and only under which, anyone can actually be *required* to furnish the TIN and make the certification for which Form W-9 is intended: Section 6109.

Sec. 6109 - Identifying numbers
(a) Supplying of identifying numbers
When required by regulations prescribed by the Secretary:
(2) Furnishing number to other persons
Any person with respect to whom a return, statement, or other document is required under the authority of

this title to be made by another person or whose identifying number is required to be shown on a return of another person shall furnish to such other person such identifying number as may be prescribed for securing his proper identification.

The pertinent regulations prescribed by the Secretary are these (with relevant portions in bold). (These are reproduced here in the order written, but the reader would do well to start with paragraph (c)):

§ *301.6109-1* Identifying numbers.

(a) In general -- (1) Taxpayer identifying numbers -- (i) Principal types. There are several types of taxpayer identifying numbers that include the following: social security numbers, Internal Revenue Service (IRS) individual taxpayer identification numbers, IRS adoption taxpayer identification numbers, and employer identification numbers.

...

(b) *Requirement to furnish one's own number -- (1) U.S. persons. Every U.S. person who makes under this title a return, statement, or other document must furnish its own taxpayer identifying number as required by the forms and the accompanying instructions.* ***A U.S. person whose number must be included on a document filed by another person must give the taxpayer identifying number so required to the other person on request.***

...

(2) *Foreign persons. The provisions of paragraph (b)(1) of this section regarding the* *furnishing of one's own number shall apply to the following foreign persons--*

(i) A foreign person that has income effectively connected with the conduct of a U.S. trade or business at any time during the taxable year;

(ii) A foreign person that has a U.S. office or place of business or a U.S. fiscal or paying agent at any time during the taxable year;

(iii) A nonresident alien treated as a resident [alien] ***under section 6013(g) or (h);***

...

(vi) A foreign person that furnishes a withholding certificate described in § 1.1441-1(e)(2) or (3) of this chapter or § 1.1441-5(c)(2)(iv) or (3)(iii) of this chapter to the extent required under § 1.1441-1(e)(4)(vii) of this chapter. [In other words, a foreign recipient who has furnished a withholding agent with a Form W-8 Certificate of Foreign Status of Beneficial Owner asserting that the "income" is actually going to someone claiming an exemption or reduced rate of tax under a tax treaty]

(c) Requirement to furnish another's number. Every person required under this title to make a return, statement, or other document must furnish such taxpayer identifying numbers of other U.S. persons

> ***and foreign persons that are described in paragraph (b)(2)(i), (ii), (iii), or (vi) of this section*** *as required by the forms and the accompanying instructions.*

(Read carefully, now. Note that there is no comma after U.S. persons in paragraph (c)-- it DOES NOT say *"...other U.S. persons, and foreign persons that are described..."*. Indeed, if that WERE what it said, it would be completely redundant, as exactly the same thing would have been said by (b) and (b)(2) et al. What (c) does say is that *only* those persons listed in (b)(2)(i), (ii), (iii), or (vi) are required to furnish a number to anyone else.)

The nature and meaning of this structure is reflected in that of the *"withholding agents"* for whose use the Form W-9 was created. Here is the last line of the Privacy Act notice found on the form's instructions:

> *Payers must generally* ***withhold 30% of taxable interest, dividend, and certain other payments*** *to a payee who does not give a TIN to a payer.*

Again, the instruction from the form itself:

> *U.S. person. Use Form W-9 only if you are a U.S. person (including a resident alien), to provide your correct TIN to the person requesting it (the requester) and, when applicable, to:*
>
> ***2. Certify that you are not subject to backup withholding,***
>
> *or*
>
> *3.* ***Claim exemption from backup withholding*** *if you are a U.S. exempt payee.*

Here is a relevant portion from the instructions for the requester:

> *Use Form W-9 to request the taxpayer identification number (TIN) of a U.S. person (including a resident alien) and to request certain certifications and claims for exemption. (See Purpose of Form on the Form W-9.)*

Withholding agents may require signed Forms W-9 from U.S. exempt recipients to overcome any presumptions of foreign status.

Now, here is the definition of a "withholding agent" and the titles of the sections to which that definition refers:

Title 26, Section 7701(a)

(16) Withholding agent

The term "withholding agent" means any person required to deduct and withhold any tax under the provisions of section 1441, 1442, 1443, or 1461.

Section 1441- Withholding of tax on nonresident aliens

Section 1442- Withholding of tax on foreign corporations

Section 1443- Foreign tax-exempt organizations

Section 1461- Liability for withheld tax

Section 1461 is the only place in Subtitle A of the IRC where anyone is 'made liable' for a tax, by the way-- here it is in its entirety:

Sec. 1461. - Liability for withheld tax

Every person required to deduct and withhold any tax under this chapter [Chapter 3 - Withholding of tax on Nonresident Aliens and Foreign Corporations -PH] *is hereby made liable for such tax and is hereby indemnified against the claims and demands of any person for the amount of any payments made in accordance with the provisions of this chapter*

So the only entities whose numbers are *required* to be included on anyone else's return (1099, etc.), and which therefore can be demanded, are three categories of foreign persons connected with a "United States" presence, "trade or business", or tax treaty; and one group of "nonresident aliens" electing*, by virtue of the provision in section 6013 (g) and (h), to be technically characterized as "resident aliens", and

therefore "U.S. persons". ***And, in all cases, only insofar as any of those entities have been paid 'income' by the filer, which is the starting point for the production of any information return.***
*The reason for the election is because the relevant law regarding nonresident aliens, primarily that originally enacted as sections 29 and 31 of the Revenue Act of 1894, and then re-enacted in subsequent legislation, provides that those so electing are entitled to the personal exemption available in the law for residents-- if they produce a return as though a resident and identify all "income" whether from sources within or without the "United States". This protocol also limits the tax to the "income" from sources "within the United States".

For the record, banks ARE required to REQUEST a number from people opening new accounts, under 31 CFR 103.34, but not for purposes of making a return; and they are considered in compliance with the all related requirements even if they don't get one, as long as they asked. Also for the record, they will usually make their request as, "We are required to ask you to execute this instrument", accurately enough. They generally won't inform their correspondent that he or she is *not* required to comply.

The many other persons who routinely demand the execution of one of these instruments from contractors and investors haven't even that regulatory excuse-- they have simply been misled to believe that they are 'required' just because they are paying someone money. However, as we have just determined, a number must only be furnished when requested by someone who is *required* to file a return-- which can only be in regard to a payment of "income", *and then* only when such a payment is made to a particular sort of person.

A great deal would seem to be being asked of a payer. Think of the litigation risks they face in unilaterally asserting that they are paying the other party "income", as well as that the other party is among the short list of persons whose number can be required. The subtextual threat that money will be withheld unless the legal instrument is executed will encourage capitulation by the requestee, but still... What are they supposed to do if the payee simply refuses to furnish a number? Violate the terms of a contract to which they've agreed? On the other hand is the risk associated with the liability imposed by section 1461 if they make a bad call the other way. How *is* the payer to know that they are paying "income" (or, if you prefer, the *"**taxable** interest, dividend, and certain other payments"* identified in the form's Privacy Act notice)? Remember, the Supreme Court has unambiguously instructed us that "income" is not to be defined as "all that comes in"; and it's not defined at all in the code...

Think back to the statutes and regulations establishing the requirements for the filings of returns which we examined in 'Crafting A Trade Or Business Plan...' and '"W" Is For Weapon' (there are a few others as well, all of precisely the same character). Recall that there is a common thread running through them: They adhere exclusively to payments made consequent to *"the performance of the functions of a public office"* ("trade or business") or of federal territorial or instrumentality origin. Now it makes sense.

The requisite knowledge supporting the *legitimate* requester's assertions is that of *their own* status, involving no guesswork or risk-- because the legitimate requester is an agent of the federal government. Only an agent of the federal government, or payer operating under the federal government's special jurisdiction, is required to file a return-- and by virtue of the same qualification, payments made from such a source *are* "income", and are not challengeable by the payee. No one else has any business demanding the submission of a W-9.

By the way, some might be wondering just what is the 30% "backup withholding" that W-9 certification protects one from. We find the answer just where we would now expect:

> *1441. Withholding of tax on nonresident aliens*
>
> *(a) General rule*
>
> *Except as otherwise provided in subsection (c), all persons, in whatever capacity acting (including lessees or mortgagors of real or personal property, fiduciaries, employers, and all officers and employees of the United States) having the control, receipt, custody, disposal, or payment of any of the items of income specified in subsection (b) (to the extent that any of such items constitutes gross income from sources within the United States), of any nonresident alien individual or of any foreign partnership shall (except as otherwise provided in regulations prescribed by the Secretary under section 874) deduct and* ***withhold from such items a tax equal to 30 percent thereof,***
>
> *Sec. 1442. Withholding of tax on foreign corporations*
>
> *(a) General rule*
>
> *In the case of foreign corporations subject to taxation under this subtitle, there shall be deducted and withheld at the source in the same manner and on the same items of income as is provided in section 1441 a* ***tax equal to 30 percent thereof.***

*****

The furnishing of a "taxpayer identification number", such as a social security number, or the execution of certain forms, amount to an implicit declaration as to either one's own status, or that of the conduct or circumstances in which the number or form is being used. If one signs a document intended for use by a "U.S. person", for instance, one is presumed to be intentionally declaring oneself as belonging to one of the several classes specified in the narrow, legal definition of that term. Similarly, if one provides an identifying number which only need be supplied by someone about whom an information return must be filed, one is implying that one's activities are of the particular legal character to which that protocol applies.

In both cases, a pretext is created for presuming that one's activities or receipts-- all of which may actually be of a purely unprivileged (and thus untaxable) character-- are legally within the ambit of the tax. Nothing which is not within the ambit of the tax *becomes* so by virtue of a mere implication, of course-- even an implication supported by the submission of a number or execution of a document such as a W-9. Such submissions and executions are merely prospective, in anticipation of circumstances that *might* obtain in the future (and which also might not). They don't transform or impose a legal character onto future events anymore than the acquisition of a fishing license makes everything the licensee does afterwards into "fishing"; and all presumptions ultimately become moot when they are resolved into claims and responses (as we will discuss in due course). Nonetheless, establishing support for these presumptions is certainly one of the main purposes behind the bureaucratic encouragement of widespread, mindless demands for the submission of W-9s.

Further, not only is a rationale created for presuming the submitters of numbers to themselves be subject to the code, but such presumptions will be subsequently used in turn against those that THEY pay, as well. The submissions will be relied upon in the future to justify treating the receipts and payments of *both* as "income".

All that said, one who is not a "U.S. person", but is facing stubborn insistence that a W-9 be submitted, could, perhaps, consider complying-- after replacing the relevant line with an accurate declaration, like: "I am a Pennsylvania citizen" (or whatever is true); and adding language such as:

> *"I have submitted this instrument solely to declare my belief that payments made to the named entity are not subject to withholding. No declaration, admission, or conclusion as to any other matter is to be presumed or understood thereby. If any law or doctrine precludes me from submitting this instrument, and/or confining its import thusly, or inflicts any infirmity or burden of any kind upon me for doing either of those things, this instrument is rescinded, null, and void."*

Obliging the requesting entity to complete the instrument itself (which we'll discuss later in 'Feeding The Hand That Bites You') might be another option.

Still, whenever possible and practical the better course is equally stubborn insistence on lawful treatment, informed by the certain knowledge that compliance as regards a W-9-- or any other legal instrument-- cannot actually be *required* under any circumstances. As the United States Supreme Court reminds us in Hale v. Henkel, 201 U.S. 43 (1906):

> *"The individual may stand upon his constitutional rights as a citizen. He is entitled to carry on his private business in his own way. His power to contract is unlimited. He owes no duty to the state or to his neighbors to divulge his business, or to open his doors to an investigation, so far as it may tend to criminate him. He owes no such duty to the state, since he receives nothing therefrom, beyond the protection of his life and property. His rights are such as existed by the law of the land long antecedent to the organization of the state, and can only be taken from him by due process of law, and in accordance with the Constitution."*

Lies, Damned Lies, And W-2's

The regulations for section 6109- *Identifying Numbers-* deal with more than just the foreign withholding provisions of the code; they also have a connection to two other "W"s used against victims of the mis-administered "income " tax-- W-2's and W-4's. These are key elements of the "employment" withholding provisions of the tax law, properly used by and about *"an officer, employee, or elected official of the United States, a State, or any political subdivision thereof, or the District of Columbia, or any agency or instrumentality of any one or more of the foregoing"*, as well as officers of federally controlled or created corporations (if they are actually paid for services rendered as corporate officers).

As with the W-9, private-sector actors not properly subject to those provisions are tricked, corrupted and intimidated into using these forms to create false evidence against themselves and others which will be subsequently relied upon by the IRS to establish an infirm legal status for such actors and a claim upon their receipts. We'll look at the W-2 and W-4 specifically, but first, the *Identifying Number* requirements regarding "employment" represent a rare thin spot in the web of deceit defending the tax scheme, and are worth a brief diversion.

Anyone who has chosen to receive the "wages" we discussed in 'Withholding The Truth' must have a number and provide it to their "employer". There is a portion of 301.6109-1(b) that directs such "employees" to a particular set of regulations just for them:

> *301.6109-1(b)(1) U.S. Persons.*
> *... For provisions dealing specifically with the duty of employees with respect to their social security numbers, see Section 31.6011(b)-2(a) and (b) of this chapter (Employment Tax Regulations). For provisions dealing specifically with the duty of employers with respect to employer identification numbers, see Section 31.6011(b)-1 of this chapter (Employment Tax Regulations).*

The referenced regulations are responsive to section 6011, which says:

> *Section 6011*
>
> > *(b) Identification of Taxpayer*
> > *The Secretary is authorized to require such information with respect to persons subject to the taxes imposed by chapter 21 or chapter 24 as is necessary or helpful in securing proper identification of such persons.*

The first set of the related regulations provide for requiring "employers" to secure and use identification numbers, in connection with W-2's, among other things, but those provisions are not relevant to this discussion. The second set addresses the use of numbers by "employees"-- and they are. This is what they say:

> *31.6011(b)-2 Employees' account numbers.*

> *(a) Requirement of application -- (1) In general --*
>
> *...*
>
> *(ii) On or after November 1, 1962. Every employee who on any day after October 31, 1962, is in employment for wages which are subject to the taxes imposed by the Federal Insurance Contributions Act or which are subject to the withholding of income tax from wages under section 3402 but who prior to such day has neither secured an account number nor made application therefore, shall make an application on Form SS-5 for* [a social security] *account number.*
>
> *(3) Furnishing of account number by employee to employer. See § 31.6109-1 for additional provisions relating to the furnishing of an account number by the employee to his employer.*

We'll look at the additional provisions in 31.6109-1 in a moment, but first note that per this regulation a SS number is REQUIRED for every "employee" in employment for "wages" or subject to withholding. (Without dwelling on it, I'll observe that the use of such qualifiers is enough to make the point by itself--if "employee" means what the IRS wants you to think it does, paragraph (ii) above would just say, " *Every employee who on any day after October 31, 1962, has neither secured an account number nor made application therefore, shall make an application on Form SS-5 for an account number.* " But read on...)

Now look at what the Social Security Administration has to say about having a social security number and working:

> *"The Social Security Act does not require a person to have an SSN to live and work in the United States, nor does it require an SSN simply for the purpose of having one. However, if someone works without an SSN, we*

cannot properly credit the earnings for the work performed."

(See the appendix for a scan of a letter in which this appears).

Here are the additional provisions at 301.6109-1 to which we were referred earlier:

301.6109-1 Identifying Numbers

...

(d) Obtaining a taxpayer identifying number--

(1) Social security number

"...Individuals who are ineligible for ***or do not wish to participate in the benefits of the social security program*** *shall nevertheless obtain a social security number if they are required to furnish such a number pursuant to paragraph (b) of this section."* [either as a foreign entity as discussed in 'W-9's...', or in connection with "employment" as outlined above].

Clearly, the law is instructing us that one does not need a number to be a worker (and get paid for it), but one does need one to be an "employee" or to receive "wages"-- ***because they're two different things***.

(By the way, simply having a Social Security number does not make one into a "taxpayer", or an "employee". Social Security is just a welfare program with a variety of arbitrary qualifying requirements, such as having been taxed for ten years with the special "income" tax discussed in 'Withholding The Truth'. A Social Security number is just the number assigned to the transcript that is associated with a particular person in which such qualifications are recorded, and remains even if such a person later goes into private-sector work. One's status is based on one's activities. To merely 'have' a Social Security number does not make someone working in the private sector into a "taxpayer" or into an "employee", any more than

having a driver's license makes someone a driver, or subject to laws regarding the use of turn signals... when he or she is just walking.)

Ok, on to W-2s...

*****

When someone begins working for "wages",

"it shall be the duty of all paymasters, and all disbursing officers, under the government of the United States, or in the employ thereof, when making any payments to officers and persons as aforesaid, or upon settling and adjusting the accounts of such officers and persons, to deduct and withhold the aforesaid duty of three per centum, and shall, at the same time, make a certificate stating the name of the officer or person from whom such deduction was made, and the amount thereof, which shall be transmitted to the office of the Commissioner of Internal Revenue, and entered as part of the internal duties;..." Section 86, Revenue Act of 1862.

The certificate to which the section refers is currently known as Form W-2. Let's look at the code language under which W-2's are to be issued (drawn from the Current Payment Tax Act of 1943 by which withholding was most recently re-enacted):

Sec. 6051. - Receipts for ***employees***

(a) Requirement

Every person ***required to deduct and withhold from an employee a tax under section 3101 or 3402,*** *or who would have been required to deduct and withhold a tax under section 3402 (determined without regard to subsection (n)) if the employee had claimed no more than one withholding exemption,* ***or every employer engaged in a trade or business who pays remuneration for services performed by an***

> ***employee**, including the cash value of such remuneration paid in any medium other than cash, shall furnish to each such employee...a written statement showing the following:*
> *(1) the name of such person,*
> *(2) the name of the employee (and his social security account number **if wages as defined in section 3121(a) have been paid),***
> *(3) the total amount of **wages as defined in section 3401(a),***
> *(4) the total amount deducted and withheld as tax under section 3402,*
> *(5) the total amount of **wages as defined in section 3121(a),***
> *(6) the total amount deducted and withheld as tax under section 3101,*
> *(d) Statements to constitute information returns*
> *A duplicate of any statement made pursuant to this section and in accordance with regulations prescribed by the Secretary shall, when required by such regulations, be filed with the Secretary.*

Recall that the *"wages as defined in section 3401(a)"* consist exclusively of remuneration paid to *"an officer, employee, or elected official of the United States, a State, or any political subdivision thereof, or the District of Columbia, or any agency or instrumentality of any one or more of the foregoing"* or *"an officer of a* [federal] *corporation".* Recall that those *"defined in section 3121(a)"* are exclusively paid for "service"; and only by the United States or a company which is resident within territory under the exclusive jurisdiction of the United States. Remember that *"every employer engaged in a trade or business"* is engaged in *"the performance of the functions of a public office".* It is clear that the restricted application of the W-2 certificate has not changed. It was and is the document used to assert payment of "income" to "employees"-- which is used today, in many cases, to make erroneous claims to that effect against private-sector 'hired' workers, just as the 1099 is similarly used against private-sector persons who work for themselves.

Once a W-2 (or 1099) has been transmitted, it is legally presumed to be honest and accurate. It is an affidavit, signed under penalty of perjury by way of the Form W-3 with which a W-2 is transmitted to the government. (The 1099-related counterpart of the W-3 is the Form 1096 transmittal document).

The payee identified on such a document will, of course, be presumed to have received taxable "income". They will be subject to all the mistreatment for which the IRS is famous, until they have either endorsed the claims of the transmitted documents-- and paid accordingly-- or have rebutted the claims as false or incorrect. The issuer of an erroneous document is also open to some government mistreatment (though only in a roundabout way)-- by being misled into committing a tort and/or crime, entirely on their own and in defiance of the clear language of the law. The penalties can be quite severe.

Here are selections of the language enumerating the potential regulatory and statutory civil liabilities of the issuer, from the Instructions for Forms W-2 and W-3, 2002 edition (emphasis is in the original):

> ***Penalties***
>
> *The following penalties generally apply to the person required to file Form W-2. The penalties apply to paper filers as well as to magnetic media/electronic filers.*
>
> ***!***
>
> *Use of a reporting agent or other third-party payroll service provider does not relieve an employer of the responsibility to ensure that Forms W-2 are furnished to employees and filed correctly and on time.*
>
> ***Failure to file correct information returns by the due date.***

If you fail to file a correct Form W-2 by the due date and cannot show reasonable cause, you may be subject to a penalty. The penalty applies if you:
- Include incorrect information on Form W-2,
*The **amount** of the penalty is based on when you file the correct Form W-2. The penalty is:*
*- **$15** per Form W-2 if you correctly file within 30 days (by March 30 if the due date is February 28); maximum penalty $75,000 per year ($25,000 for small businesses, defined later).*
*- **$30** per Form W-2 if you correctly file more than 30 days after the due date but by August 1; maximum penalty $150,000 per year ($50,000 for small businesses).*
*- **$50** per Form W-2 if you file after August 1 or you do not file required Forms W-2; maximum penalty $250,000 per year ($100,000 for small businesses).*
!
*If you **do not** file corrections and you do not meet any of the exceptions to the penalty stated below, the penalty is **$50** per information return.*
***Exceptions to the penalty.** The following are exceptions to the failure to file penalty:*
***1.** The penalty will not apply to any failure that you can show was due to **reasonable cause** and not to willful neglect. In general, you must be able to show that your failure was due to an event beyond your control or due to significant mitigating factors. You must also be able to show that you acted in a responsible manner and took steps to avoid the failure.*
***2.** An **inconsequential error or omission** is not considered a failure to include correct information.*
Errors and omissions that are never inconsequential are those relating to:
***c.** Any money amounts.*

Intentional disregard of filing requirements. *If any failure to file a correct Form W-2 is due to intentional disregard of the filing or correct information requirements, the penalty is at least $100 per Form W-2 with no maximum penalty.*

Failure to furnish correct payee statements. *If you fail to provide correct payee statements (Forms W-2) to your employees and you cannot show reasonable cause, you may be subject to a penalty. The penalty applies if you fail to provide the statement by January 31, you fail to include all information required to be shown on the statement, or you include incorrect information on the statement.*

The penalty is $50 per statement, no matter when the correct statement is furnished, with a maximum of $100,000 per year.

The penalty is not reduced for furnishing a correct statement by August 1.

Exception. *An inconsequential error or omission is not considered a failure to include correct information. An inconsequential error or omission cannot reasonably be expected to prevent or hinder the payee from timely receiving correct information and reporting it on his or her income tax return or from otherwise putting the statement to its intended use.*

Errors and omissions that are never inconsequential are those relating to:

1. *A dollar amount,*

Intentional disregard of payee statement requirements.

If any failure to provide a correct payee statement (Form W-2) to an employee is due to intentional disregard of the requirements to furnish a correct payee statement, the penalty is at least $100 per Form W-2 with no maximum penalty.

> ***Civil damages for fraudulent filing of Forms W-2.*** *If you willfully file a fraudulent Form W-2 for payments you claim you made to another person, that person may be able to sue you for damages. You may have to pay $5,000 or more.* [Pursuant to IRC section 7434]

Here is the language of section 7434, which applies to erroneous 1099's as well as W-2's:

> *Sec. 7434. - Civil damages for fraudulent filing of information returns*
>
> *(a) In general*
>
> *If any person willfully files a fraudulent information return with respect to payments purported to be made to any other person, such other person may bring a civil action for damages against the person so filing such return.*
>
> *(b) Damages*
>
> *In any action brought under subsection (a), upon a finding of liability on the part of the defendant, the defendant shall be liable to the plaintiff in an amount equal to the greater of $5,000 or the sum of -*
>
> *(1)*
>
> *any actual damages sustained by the plaintiff as a proximate result of the filing of the fraudulent information return (including any costs attributable to resolving deficiencies asserted as a result of such filing),*
>
> *(2)*
>
> *the costs of the action, and*
>
> *(3)*
>
> *in the court's discretion, reasonable attorneys' fees.*

As the W-2 penalty provisions are arguably confined in application to *"the person required to file form W-2"* (known to you, O educated reader, to be a specialized 'person'), the one that counts the most is that very last paragraph regarding section 7434 civil liability to the listed payee for filing a fraudulent information return alleging payments made to another person. It is also the most artistic. The scheme undertakes numbingly complicated measures to fool a private company into the belief that they MUST file these forms falsely declaring their workers and contractors to be being paid in connection with the conduct of a public office, and then quietly acknowledges that if they do so, they can be sued by the aggrieved parties.

Understand clearly that this *is* the character of that last element of the penalty notice. It is making false claims of *payments made to* the listed person, **not** *payments made on behalf of* that person that are addressed here. In other words, this notice refers to the filing of a form by a company claiming to have paid *"wages as defined in 3401 or 3121"* or *"gains, profits or income"* in the course of a *"trade or business"* to a person when in fact they did not. A company making false claims regarding *how much tax they withheld and paid to the IRS on behalf of someone* answers to the government for the mistake by way of the other penalties listed above (and possibly for perjury as well). The worker is always credited with any amount withheld as tax under section 31, even if the money was never paid by the withholding company-- and liability for such amounts remains with the company, under section 3403.

The statutory 7434 liability to a worker or contractor with regard to whom a false W-2 or 1099 is filed is a risk in addition to that of common-law liability to that same person for all the money being improperly withheld, of course, along with any costs of action; and any other penalties provided by law for the making of unauthorized deductions from pay, which are provided under many union state codes. Furthermore, impersonating a federal official or employee, as in pretending to be engaged in the performance of the functions of a public office and withholding from one's "employees" accordingly, is a felony under 18 USC 912:

> *Sec. 912. - Officer or employee of the United States*
> *Whoever falsely assumes or pretends to be an officer or employee acting under the authority of the United States or any department, agency or officer thereof, and acts as such, or in such pretended character demands or obtains any money, paper, document, or thing of value, shall be fined under this title or imprisoned not more than three years, or both.*

Needless to say, the private company undertaking all these risks is presumed to be fully familiar with the law, and is doing what it is doing entirely on its own. As we noted previously, the government and its agencies are careful not to cross the line into commanding illegality-- they content themselves with the generally satisfactory consequences of private misunderstanding, incompetent professional assistance and an abiding, deeply planted and frequently watered fear of acting contrary to what the widely-reputed-to-be-rogue-and-dangerous agency appears to want.

This is not to say that the tax-collection engine is complacent, of course. Substantial and sophisticated measures are taken to support the errors of understanding which contribute to the process. Among these is always presumptively referring to all workers as "employees". If asked, the IRS or its industry allies will always declare that, "All employees are subject to withholding,". They will not make such a statement when inaccuracy carries a risk of liability, such as over a personal signature, or under oath, without adding the qualifier regarding the definition of "employees". You will notice, if you have occasion to have much contact with this agency, that they will NEVER say "All workers are subject to withholding", or, "Everyone who works for you is subject to withholding" (unless the questioner is engaged in a "trade or business", of course).

They will run a malicious "Who's on first?" routine with the unsuspecting: "Do I have to withhold from my workers?" "Are they your employees?" "Uh, I guess so..." "Then you have to withhold from them!"

Communications sent from the IRS to businesses (and workers) will always be constructed to mislead. The most egregious and pernicious example of this is the Form 688-W Notice of Levy by which the agency seeks to co-opt a company into committing theft-by-conversion by sending it part of a workers pay in the absence of a court order to do so. This form not only repeatedly refers to its target as an "employee", inviting agreement by acquiescence, but it includes extended excerpts from Section 6331 of the IRC, concerning Levy and Distraint, on its back, allowing those excerpts to imply authority for the requested seizure. The careful observer will notice, however, that the excerpts start with subparagraph (b) of that section.

> *(b) Seizure and sale of property*
> *The term "levy" as used in this title includes the power of distraint and seizure by any means. Except as otherwise provided in subsection (e), a levy shall extend only to property possessed and obligations existing at the time thereof. In any case in which the Secretary may levy upon property or rights to property, he may seize and sell such property or rights to property (whether real or personal, tangible or intangible).*

Here is the subparagraph (a) which is deliberately left out:

> *(a) Authority of Secretary--If any person liable to pay any tax neglects or refuses to pay the same within 10 days after notice and demand, it shall be lawful for the Secretary to collect such tax (and further sum as shall be sufficient to cover the expenses of the levy) by levy upon all property and rights to property (except such*

> *property as is exempt under section 6334) belonging to such person or on which there is a lien provided in this chapter for the payment of such tax.* ***Levy may be made upon the accrued salary or wages of any officer, employee, or elected official, of the United States, the District of Columbia, or any agency or instrumentality of the United States or the District of Columbia, by serving a notice of levy on the employer (as defined in section 3401(d)) of such officer, employee, or elected official.*** *If the Secretary makes a finding that the collection of such tax is in jeopardy, notice and demand for immediate payment of such tax may be made by the Secretary and, upon failure or refusal to pay such tax, collection thereof by levy shall be lawful without regard to the 10-day period provided in this section. (Emphasis added).*

Documents like the "Notice of Levy", when improperly sent to a private-sector company, end with a *"Thank you for your cooperation"*. This expression is sincere. Without a private-sector company's cooperation, in withholding and/or sending other people's lawlessly demanded money AND accepting all the legal risk for the lawsuit and possible criminal charges, the IRS would never see an unprivileged, private-sector dime. And let's never forget, Congress set them up with their quite good-paying jobs (which are financed out of the take) for no purpose except to bring in every penny on which they can get their hands.

W-4's- The Blind Leading The Blind Down A Primrose Path

The essence of the income tax as it is administered is fraud, pure and simple. It is what is known as "constructive fraud", meaning that while it may not be possible to readily identify a smoking gun of overt, unambiguous offense, what is nonetheless accomplished by the scheme is a victim's loss and a beneficiary's gain. All the same, the perpetrators of the scheme retain defensive deniability because the law contains the truth about the voluntary character of the tax-- anyone who goes to the trouble can read it for themselves. But, being the cheap con that it is, the scheme introduces itself to most of its victims under circumstances in which they are least likely to go to that trouble, understand the legal implications of their own acts or the limitations to which the government is subject, or insist on being dealt with lawfully.

Furthermore, this introduction is actually carried out through the offices of a third party-- a private business-- which typically has itself been suckered or intimidated into being the scheme's foil. Consequently, legal liability falls on that third party, rather than the principal actors in the scheme. We'll discuss this more in the next section.

The first taste of the "income" tax scheme comes to most people at a tender age and while in a vulnerable state, as a little innocent-looking form called a W-4, presented to them as a prerequisite to satisfying the powerful desire to secure their first real job. Not only is everything related to that process new and mysterious, but only a truly rare 16- or 18-year-old kid would think or dare to question the matter-of-factly delivered instructions to fill out this form, titled the *"Employee's Withholding Allowance Certificate"*, in order to start work. Those few that would even take the trouble to read what they were signing would find this carefully selected language accompanying the form, explaining that,

> *Purpose. Complete Form W-4 so that your employer can withhold the correct Federal income tax from your pay. Because your tax situation may change, you may want to refigure your withholding each year.*

and,

> *Privacy Act and Paperwork Reduction Act Notice. We ask for the information on this form to carry out the Internal Revenue laws of the United States. The Internal Revenue Code requires this information under sections 3402(f)(2)(A) and 6109 and their regulations. Failure to provide a properly completed form will result in your being treated as a single person who claims no withholding allowances; providing fraudulent information may also subject you to penalties.*

Somehow, the language of section 3402(f)(2)(A) and 6109 are left off the form. We looked at 6109 in detail in the last two sections; here is the language of 3402(f)(2)(A):

> *Sec. 3402. - Income tax collected at source*
>
> *(f)...*
>
> *(2) Exemption certificates*

> *(A) On commencement of employment*
> *On or before the date of the commencement of employment with an **employer**, the **employee** shall furnish the **employer** with a signed withholding exemption certificate relating to the number of withholding exemptions which he claims, which shall in no event exceed the number to which he is entitled.*

Recall once again the definitions of the key terms in this section (discussed in detail in 'Withholding The Truth'):

> *(c) Employee*
> *For purposes of this chapter, the term "employee" includes an officer, employee, or elected official of the United States, a State, or any political subdivision thereof, or the District of Columbia, or any agency or instrumentality of any one or more of the foregoing. The term "employee" also includes an officer of a corporation.*
> *(d) Employer*
> *For purposes of this chapter, the term "employer" means the person for whom an individual performs or performed any service, of whatever nature, as the employee of such person...*

It is obvious that in the case of this form, as in so much else associated with the "income" tax, any requirement of execution, and adverse consequences of declining to do so, are restricted in their application to federal and "State" government workers exclusively.

Nonetheless, I think it is safe to say that most teenagers raising this point with the Human Resources department where they've just been offered their first job are likely to find themselves labeled a troublemaker and out pounding the pavement again. That's unless they are successfully browbeaten with an impatient, "Look, kid, you're signing on to be an employee, right? You're going to be paid wages, right? The law says all employees getting paid wages have to fill out one of these forms. Whaddayamean you're not an "employee"! Lemme see that! Oh,... I see why you're confused. You didn't notice that it says *includes* officers and employees, etc., etc.. That means that it includes *anybody else* who's an employee, too, and *anybody* who works for *anybody* is an EM-PLOY-EE! *Understand?* Trust me. Fill out the form. And stop talking to those tax-protestor nutcases."

With most of the "income" tax forms of this type, what has been said so far would cover the subject well enough, at least as regards the applicability of the instrument to private-sector workers, and I could keep this part of the book short. The W-4 is a bit more complicated, however, perhaps in the interest of pacifying the rare, legally knowledgeable cat's-paw business upon which the scheme is so reliant. As such a business might otherwise fear the legal consequences of unlawfully demanding the form as a condition for fulfilling the obligations of the contract into which it has entered with a worker, or be cognizant of the consequences of pretending to be a federal official (the only entity in connection with which a W-4 could be required), the law regarding the W-4 is equipped with what appears to be a "safe harbor" element. That element is subparagraph (p)(3)(B) of section 3402. Here it is (with emphasis added):

> *Sec. 3402. - Income tax collected at source*
> *(p)* ***Voluntary withholding agreements***
> *(3) Authority for other voluntary withholding*
>> ***The Secretary is authorized by regulations to provide for withholding***

> *(A) from remuneration for services performed by an employee for the employee's employer which (without regard to this paragraph) does not constitute wages, and*
> *(B)* ***from any other type of payment*** *with respect to which the Secretary finds that withholding would be appropriate under the provisions of this chapter, if the employer and employee, or the* ***person making and the person receiving such other type of payment, agree to such withholding****. Such agreement shall be in such form and manner as the Secretary may by regulations prescribe.* ***For purposes of this chapter (and so much of subtitle F as relates to this chapter), remuneration or other payments with respect to which such agreement is made shall be treated as if they were wages paid by an employer to an employee to the extent that such remuneration is paid or other payments are made during the period for which the agreement is in effect.*** (I'm confident that we can all easily think of dozens of *'other types of payments'* regarding which we would be grateful for the benefits of this provision of the law, right?)

By virtue of this provision, a nervous private-sector company might still cooperate with the scheme, presuming that it can claim it just thought it was agreeing to an optional request to withhold when accepting that W-4 and handing over to a third party money owed to a worker.

However, despite the language of 3402(p)(3)(B), the Secretary of the Treasury has promulgated *no* regulations providing for any particular "form or manner" of agreement between a "person" and another "person" (although he *has* provided several pages of such regulations for voluntary withholding agreements between "employees" and "employers" pursuant to 3402(p)(3)(A)). Therefore, the characterization of payments made to a worker as being subject to withholding is-- wishful thinking to the contrary notwithstanding-- entirely the doing, and the risk, of the business doing the withholding. The poorly constructed language of the statute only provides for the possibility of this extra-curricular withholding pursuant to a regulatory structure-- lacking such, it is a mere will-o'-the-wisp.

Though perhaps a bit disingenuously, a worker could and would easily and credibly maintain, in the course of suing or prosecuting a business over what is no more or less than theft-by-conversion, that in addition to responding to the coercion and false claims of authority by which she was induced to execute the form, she at bottom complied because of the reasonable presumption that the W-4 would only become an active instrument if and when the business's affairs contrived to cause her pay to be effectively connected with a taxable activity. That the business instead withheld from her private-sector, untaxable receipts is entirely its own responsibility.

Needless to say, and despite 3402(p)(3)(B), the fact that a business calls payments "wages" paid to an "employee"-- and even reports them as such-- does not transform them into "income", if they are actually paid to a private-sector worker. Chapter 24 imposes no tax at all (nor does subtitle F)-- it simply provides for withholding. The amounts withheld under its provisions are credited against any liability for "income" tax which might be found to exist under the provisions of subtitle A-- in regard to which, as we know, remuneration for private-sector work is explicitly excluded. (We'll explore this area in detail later when we look at what the law says about refunds.)

*****

Possible rationales for its completion and submission do not change the fact that a signed W-4 becomes an instrument supporting treatment of a worker as being a "wage"-paid-"employee". Through this form, the company for whom the victim works is provided not simply a pretext for withholding and diverting part of the money it owes to that victim (otherwise illegal if objected to-- absent a court order); but also a pretext for issuing a related W-2 at the end of the year. This in turn supplies the IRS with *its* excuse to presume that the individual in question is a government "employee", whose pay is therefore "income" upon which taxes can lawfully be demanded.

Anyone currently working for others who has been forced or fooled into improperly submitting a W-4 might wish to withdraw the authority to withhold that the form represents, by filing an appropriately worded instrument with their personnel department, such as this:

TERMINATION OF AUTHORITY TO WITHHOLD

(Company's Name) is notified hereby that I, ___(Worker's Name)___, am declaring ended and withdrawn as of this date, ___(Today's Date)___, any and all authorization and/or agreement for the withholding of any portion of compensation owed me for services rendered howsoever such authorization and/or agreement may have been conveyed, executed, or implied at any time.

____

____/____/____

Because an agreement between a non-"employee" and a non-"employer" regarding withholding is neither regulated nor required, one can end it at any time by simply withdrawing any implied or explicit permission.

(Those being coerced to execute a new W-4 might wish to consider a disclaimer similar to the one that can be seen at www.losthorizons.com/appendix.htm. Simply filing "Exempt" is not a proper strategy, by the way, nor legal-- *all* the provisions of law relating to W-4's apply only to "employees", including that one. 'Exempt' does not mean "under no obligation", it means "conditionally released or excepted from obligation".)

Feeding The Hand That Bites You

"We must note here, as a matter of judicial knowledge, that most lawyers have only scant knowledge of tax law."
Bursten v. U.S., 395 F 2d 976, 981 (5th Cir. 1968)

I mentioned in the last section that the private-sector businesses who are co-opted into facilitating various elements of the scheme which are ultimately directed at others, such as executing W-2's and demanding the execution of W-9's and W-4's, have been compromised themselves early on. It is worth our while to discuss how this is done, for despite being complicit as nearly the sole force subjecting workers to the mal-administration of the "income" tax, such businesses are themselves victims (at least, to begin with), and not only as the liable actor open to bureaucratic and criminal penalties, as well as civil suits.

For instance, a typical company suckered into participating in the scheme is subjecting itself to as much as a 13.85% tax on the first $7,000 of every workers pay, and 7.65% on the most of the rest-- its "share" of "employment taxes" and the federal "unemployment" tax-- for which it is otherwise not legally liable, as we discussed in 'Withholding The Truth'. There is also, of course, a very considerable cost in the form of administrative expenses associated with such participation.

By one estimate, Americans spend 5.4 billion hours, at an annual cost of $600 billion to the economy, just completing the paperwork requirements of federal taxes (James L. Payne, "Unhappy Returns: The $600 Billion Tax Rip-Off," *Policy Review,* Winter 1992, pp. 18–22). Businesses bear 52.4% of that cost, despite being a small minority of filers, according to The Tax Foundation, in its February, 2002 report "The Cost of Tax Compliance". (That report pegs the man-hour total at a higher figure still, and observes that, "Put another way, 5.8 billion hours per year represents a work force of over 2,774,000 people, larger than the populations of Dallas (1,189,000), Detroit (951,000) and Washington, D.C. (572,000) combined, and more people than work in the agricultural industry (1.14 million), the automobile manufacturing industry (1.013 million), the computer manufacturing industry (355,830), hardware stores (170,360) and museums and art galleries (82,410) combined. This is also more people than would reside in four Congressional districts.").

These quantifiable costs are the visible expenses imposed by the scheme. The hidden costs are more significant still, and go well beyond just the opportunity costs which parallel any involuntary expenditure. These are the costs imposed in the form of regulatory busy-bodying-- the dictating of form, process, etc., in a thick, expensive and suffocating cloud of such density and scope as to be beyond description here, but which will be well known to anyone in business for themselves or to those working for others in roles of a certain sort.

Virtually all of these burdens are made possible by the river of wealth diverted into the hands of government by the "income" tax scheme. There is a direct correlation between the growth curve of the micro-managing regulatory state and that of the scheme bringing in the means by which the requisite army of bureaucrats is hired and maintained. Without sorting among such burdens to pick those of which anyone might or should individually approve or disapprove, all are illegitimate to the degree that they are made possible through fraud, coercion, or subterfuge.

This larger issue, which as much as anything amounts to the general erosion of the rule of law, brings harm to the business community with a certain poetic justice. Having quietly let stand unchallenged a million un- (or at least ill-) founded claims of government power over the last 90 years despite being uniquely equipped with the wherewithal to fight back-- either for the sake of expediency or from being corrupted with a piece of the action-- these same business owners are now the permanent victims of the state through ever-greater peregrinations by Congress and the executive.

Almost completely unleashed by these repeated capitulations to its taking of liberties with the law (!), the government preys upon them more or less at will in the service of the political and remunerative interests of its beneficiaries. The form that these predations take-- the extraction of fines, legal concessions and control over policy-- enlarge, entrench and embolden the political support for such practices. The courts, habituated by both convention and the typical jurist's natural reluctance to swim against the tide, are generally willing to remain silent when the similarly motivated counsel for the latest victim declines to argue against the state's creative usurpations.

Nonetheless, every January thousands of businesses across the country pause their year-long efforts to generate and protect revenue. They take a break from the often contentious (and always expensive and resented) daily struggle to fight-- or avoid ruin in surrendering to-- the all-too-frequently lawless dictates issued by those millions of highly paid (and otherwise idle) federal and state bureaucrats as to the conduct of their affairs. They tell their crack defensive legal teams, which in all other cases are under strict instructions to painstakingly research the intricacies of the law, to go out for coffee. Then these businesses spend a few quiet moments on self-destruction.

Obediently, and without a fuss, they participate in the annual fraud that finances those same bureaucratic infringements. Obediently, and without a fuss, these businesses sign and issue millions of sworn, but false, affidavits specifically declaring their private-sector workers to have been paid government "wages". Obediently and without a fuss they create the legal fictions through which the federal and state governments steal some 2 trillion or so dollars and replenish the lifeblood of the assault against which these businesses battle for their survival the other 364 days of the year. In all twelve months of the year, every time they hire a new worker or pay a contractor, they will similarly throw food to their tormentors.

Why?

Well, one of the first things that the founders of new businesses will do is to march proudly to the bank to open a checking account with which to pay suppliers and workers and to process incoming receipts. One of the first things the friendly and helpful bank "employee" with whom they deal will do is ask, "Is this a business account? Yes? Well, then, what is your Employer Identification Number (EIN)?" If one hasn't been executed already, they will produce a Form SS-4, by which the naïve new business customer can create a legal presumption that theirs is the sort of entity in need of such a number. In the interim during which the newly submitted form is being processed, the bank will be happy to use the owner's social security number instead; but no account will be opened without a number.

We've already looked at the limited legal requirements of having and furnishing a number to others in connection to W-9's and "employment" in previous sections. Here is the remaining statutory language relating to having a number at all:

> *Sec. 6109. - Identifying numbers*
>
> *(a) Supplying of identifying numbers*
>
> > *When required by regulations prescribed by the Secretary:*
> >
> > *(1) Inclusion in returns*
> >
> > > *Any person* ***required under the authority of this title to make a return, statement, or other document*** *shall include in such return, statement, or other document such identifying number as may be prescribed for securing proper identification of such person.*

Now, disregarding the special groups previously examined and those in the alcohol, tobacco, or firearms businesses (for all of whom special statutory assignments of liability and requirements for returns apply), here is the general statutory requirement to make a return:

> *Sec. 6012. - Persons required to make returns of income*
>
> *(a) General rule*
>
> > *Returns with respect to income taxes under subtitle A shall be made by the following:*
> >
> > *(1)*
> >
> > > *(A)*
> > >
> > > *Every individual* ***having for the taxable year gross income which equals or exceeds the exemption amount****,...* (what follows is essentially a series of exceptions to the requirement).

Clearly, the general requirement to make a return, and therefore have a number, is as much dependent upon specialized, federally-connected circumstances as are the more particular requirements at which we have looked before.

This is all consistently expressed in the instructions for the Form SS-4 (Application for an Employer Identification Number):

> *Do I Need an EIN?*
> *File Form SS-4 if the applicant entity does not already have an EIN but is required to show an EIN on any return, statement, or other document. For example, a sole proprietorship or self-employed farmer who establishes a qualified retirement plan, or is required to file excise, employment, alcohol, tobacco, or firearms returns, must have an EIN. A partnership, corporation, REMIC (real estate mortgage investment conduit), nonprofit organization (church, club, etc.), or farmers' cooperative must use an EIN for any tax-related purpose even if the entity does not have employees.*

(By now, every reader will have immediately noted that this instruction does **not** simply say, *"File Form SS-4 if your business does not already have an EIN."*)

The application says in its required Privacy Act notice that:

> *We ask for the information on this form to carry out the Internal Revenue laws of the United States. We need it to comply with section 6109 and the regulations thereunder, which generally require the inclusion of an employer identification number (EIN) on certain returns, statements, or other documents filed with the Internal Revenue Service.*

Compelled by the bank's intransigence (or that of a client demanding the completion of a W-9), the new entrepreneur will file the SS-4 and ask for a number -- helped

About 1040's, And Claiming Refunds

ꟹ

"The revenue laws are a code or system in regulation of tax assessment and collection. They relate to taxpayers, and not to nontaxpayers. The latter are without their scope." United States Court of Claims, Economy Plumbing and Heating v. United States, 470 F.2d 585, at 589 (1972)

It's time to expand our vocabularies with another custom term that most honest persons would (and do) automatically presume to have a common, logical meaning, but which is, in fact, another narrowly-defined legal term stealthily deployed in furtherance of the "income" tax scheme... "taxpayer". Like all such terms, it is created and used for very deliberate reasons (among which is *not* brevity or clarity).

> *Internal Revenue Code, Section 7701(a)(14): Taxpayer: The term 'taxpayer' means any person subject to any internal revenue tax.*

We're all accustomed to the use of the normal term 'tax-payer', typically deployed in a, "Hey, how about some service here?! I'm a tax-payer, you know!" or, "Listen, Bub, I'm a tax-payer. I'm one of the people that pays your salary!" sort of way. This benign, descriptive term is generally used interchangeably with "adult citizen". The custom legal term "taxpayer" is easily mistaken for this normal, common language homonym-- indeed, as with most such terms within the "income" tax scheme, a determined effort is constantly underway to encourage exactly that mistake-- but it is a grave and widely misleading error.

Subject to: Liable, subordinate, subservient, inferior, obedient to; governed or affected by; provided that; provided; answerable for. Homan v. Employers Reinsurance Corp., 345 Mo. 650, 136 S.W. 2d 289, 302 Black's Law Dictionary, 5th edition.

As we learn by examining the key element in the definition of "taxpayer", the term actually means, "a person liable (obligated) for an internal revenue tax" such as "income" taxes and certain other specific excises involving alcohol, tobacco, etc. Thus, despite paying fuel taxes, airport taxes, property taxes, alcohol taxes, tobacco taxes-- in fact, hundreds of federal taxes (for all of which liability falls on the vendor)-- the vast majority of adult American citizens are not "taxpayers", because they are not "employers", "withholding agents", recipients of "income" in more than the exemption amount, or other such specialized entities by virtue of which liability for an internal revenue tax might arise.

Of course, the IRS sees and describes such citizens differently, perhaps in order to secure, through a lack of protest to the application of the term, more presumptive evidence regarding the status of intended targets. Also, of course, partly because the agency's only awareness of any given person is through documents such as those we have discussed throughout this part of 'Cracking the Code', which, if accurate, would mean that they WERE a "taxpayer".

Far and away the largest part of the tax law, and particularly the administrative portion at which we will be looking now, addresses and affects only those who are "taxpayers". But there are certain sections, and parts of sections, that are written with others in mind. These are often distinguishable solely by the quiet substitution of 'person' or 'individual' etc., where "taxpayer" is otherwise typically used. Because such sections are almost seamlessly intermingled with preceding and succeeding sections which reference-- and exclusively apply to-- "taxpayers", it is easy to misunderstand and imagine that the 'persons' to which the odd portion refers are obliged or restricted by the "taxpayer only" portions, when this is not the case. We will be observing this distinction in key places as we now proceed.

(An ongoing sensitivity to this nuance is also important. Any non-"taxpayer" implementing what we are about to discuss is likely to encounter stubborn IRS efforts to steer them into frustrating administrative procedures and requirements solely provided for, and appropriate to, "taxpayers". It is critical to know, in such circumstances, that any commands incorporating language such as, "The taxpayer shall..." don't apply and are, in fact, virtually guaranteed to be counterproductive.)

*****

Since the beginning of the "income" tax, provision has been made by which an entity (an individual, company, etc.) can make a legal statement regarding its receipts-- either to pro-actively announce otherwise unrecorded "income" or to address by confirmation, rebuttal or modification the declarations of others regarding those receipts. Here is the original language of this provision:

Sec. 93. And be it further enacted, That it shall be the duty of all persons of lawful age, and all guardians and trustees, whether such trustees are so by virtue of their office as executors, administrators, or other fiduciary capacity, to make returns in the list or schedule, as provided in this act, to the proper officer of internal revenue, of the amount of his or her income, or the income of such minors or persons as may be held in trust as aforesaid, according to the requirements hereinbefore stated, and in case of neglect or refusal to make such return, the assessor or assistant assessor shall assess the amount of his or her income, and proceed thereafter to collect the duty thereon in the same manner as is provided for in other cases of neglect or refusal to furnish lists or schedules in the general provisions of this act, where not otherwise incompatible, and the assistant assessor may increase the amount of the list or return of any party making such return, if he shall be satisfied that the same is understated: Provided, that any party, in his or her own behalf, or as guardian or trustee, as aforesaid, shall be permitted to declare, under oath or affirmation, the form and manner of which shall be prescribed by the Commissioner of Internal Revenue, that he or she was not possessed of an income of six hundred dollars, liable to be assessed according to the provisions of this act, or that he or she has been assessed elsewhere and the same year for an income duty, under authority of the United States, and shall thereupon be exempt from an income duty; or, if the list or return of any party shall have been increased by the assistant assessor, in manner as aforesaid, he or she may be permitted to declare, as aforesaid, the amount of his or her annual income, or the amount held in trust, as aforesaid, liable to be assessed, as aforesaid, and the same so declared shall be received as the sum upon which duties are to be assessed and collected.

The condensed version of this section is: Everyone must make a return assessing appropriate taxes on their "income", if they had more than the exemption amount. The government is authorized to make a return from its own knowledge in cases of neglect or refusal, or to increase an understated return based upon such knowledge-- but in either case, an affidavit regarding the amount of such "income" executed by the affected party is the final word on the matter. The government is authorized to assess the taxes due on whatever that final "income" figure proves to be. Note that there is no practical downside to neglecting to make a return for anyone whose "income" is below the exemption amount-- in the worst case, an erroneous assertion to the contrary by the government is simply answered by a corrective return, and the matter is finished.

This provision is unchanged in the current code:

Sec. 6012. - Persons required to make returns of income

(a) General rule

Returns with respect to income taxes under subtitle A shall be made by the following:

(1)

(A) Every individual having for the taxable year gross income which equals or exceeds the exemption amount [currently $2000 -PH]

Sec. 6020. - Returns prepared for or executed by Secretary

(a) Preparation of return by Secretary

If any person shall fail to make a return required by this title or by regulations prescribed thereunder, but shall consent to disclose all information necessary for the

> *preparation thereof, then, and in that case, the Secretary may prepare such return, which, being signed by such person, may be received by the Secretary as the return of such person.*
>
> *Sec. 6201. - Assessment authority*
> *(a) Authority of Secretary*
> *The Secretary is authorized and required to make the inquiries, determinations, and assessments of all taxes (including interest, additional amounts, additions to the tax, and assessable penalties) imposed by this title, or accruing under any former internal revenue law, which have not been duly paid by stamp at the time and in the manner provided by law. Such authority shall extend to and include the following:*
>
> *(1) Taxes shown on return*
>
> *The Secretary shall assess all taxes determined by the taxpayer or by the Secretary as to which returns or lists are made under this title.* [If one declares enough "income" to owe taxes thereon, one is a "taxpayer" -PH]

As prescribed in the 1862 act, the current section 6012 requires a return only from someone who has determined themselves to have "income" of [currently] $2000 or more in a given year. Section 6020(a) provides that the Secretary of the Treasury is authorized to prepare a substitute for an unmade or allegedly incorrect required return, based upon the declarations of the person with whom it is concerned, which, if signed (subscribed) by that person becomes the final return. Section 6201 describes the authority of the Secretary to determine (calculate) and assess taxes if the requisite amount of "income" has been specified by the citizen-- who thus becomes a "taxpayer"-- on either type of return. (I'll restate this last element, because it is important and frequently misunderstood: 6201 provides authority only for the Secretary to assess the tax, not to determine the amount of "income" upon which the tax is imposed. These are two entirely separate and fundamentally different things.)

So, down through the years, one of the primary functions of a Form 1040 is unchanged: The making of a *legally definitive* statement as to amount of "income", either proactively or reactively, and either by or on behalf of, a citizen. The law still provides no authority by which the government is empowered to override the definitive assertion of a private, non-governmentally-connected citizen as to amount of "income" received.

In such a case, after all, the government is only a potential beneficiary. It has no personal knowledge of the facts or other legal standing. Because of the structure of the scheme, it can have an active role as a biased intermediary in a dispute involving one party's erroneous documentary assertions regarding the "income" of another party. However, despite rooting and shilling for the one side and trying to browbeat the other, the government has nothing but hot air to bring to the contest, which it is doomed to lose to a determined and informed citizen. No flurry of allegations is sufficiently large to make Joe's Auto Repair into the Department of Transportation.

The government *can* contest the assertions of actual federal and "State" officers and "employees" though, because as the paymaster, the government itself has direct, personal knowledge of the facts-- it is itself one of the parties in the "income" transaction-- and it has standing as a contracting party. Subsection (b) of section 6020 reflects this relationship:

> *Sec. 6020. - Returns prepared for or executed by Secretary*
>
> *(b) Execution of return by Secretary*

(1) Authority of Secretary to execute return

If any person fails to make any return required by any internal revenue law or regulation made thereunder at the time prescribed therefor, or makes, willfully or otherwise, a false or fraudulent return, the Secretary shall make such return ***from his own knowledge*** *and from such information as he can obtain through testimony or otherwise.*

(2) Status of returns

Any return so made ***and subscribed by the Secretary*** *shall be prima facie good and sufficient for all legal purposes*

("prima facie means, *"Evidence that is sufficient to raise a presumption of fact or to establish the fact in question unless rebutted."*"Lectric Law Library; *"a fact presumed to be true unless disproved by some evidence to the contrary."* Black's Law Dictionary, 6th edition)

Quite differently from the authority provided in 6020(a), 6020(b) provides for the creation of a required return by the Secretary based upon *his own knowledge of the facts,* which, if such a return is signed under penalty of perjury, becomes a legally sufficient (but still rebuttable) return.

Take special note that the statute does not provide that the Secretary may make such a return based upon, *"his own knowledge* ***<u>or</u>*** *from such information as he can obtain through testimony or otherwise."* The statute specifically requires that the Secretary of the Treasury draw upon his own (institutional) knowledge. Indeed, how else can he or his delegate declare under penalty of perjury that to the best of their knowledge and belief the information on the document so created is true and complete? A return is not a transcription of hearsay allegations, the accurate recording of which is being attested to by the signer. It is an affidavit reflecting the signer's own testimony.

It is not necessary for 6020(b) or any other statute to expressly reveal the narrowness of its scope due to the limitation of the Secretary's legal standing, or explain how that limitation is invoked by the *"from his own knowledge"* language. The law, rightly or wrongly, assumes understanding of these nuances in the reader. However, in this particular case the Secretary's own regulatory material acknowledges this limitation, and thus confirms it quite clearly. Here are the instructions furnished to IRS personnel regarding the authority of the IRS to make substitute returns (from the year 2007 Internal Revenue Manual):

> 5.1.11.6.8 (03-01-2007)
> *IRC 6020(b) Authority*
> *1. The following returns may be prepared, signed and assessed under the authority of IRC 6020(b):*
> *A. Form 940, Employer's Annual Federal Unemployment Tax Return*
> *B. Form 941, Employer's Quarterly Federal Tax Return*
> *C. Form 942, Employer's Quarterly Tax Return for Household Employees*
> *D. Form 943, Employer's Annual Tax Return for Agricultural Employees*
> *E. Form 720, Quarterly Federal Excise Tax Return*
> *F. Form 2290, Heavy Vehicle Use Tax Return*
> *G. Form CT-1, Employer's Annual Railroad Retirement Tax Return*
> *H. Form 1065, U.S. Partnership Return of Income*
>
> *2. The following are authorized to execute returns under IRC 6020(b):*
> *A. Revenue officers.*

> *B. Automated Collection System (ACS) and Collection Support function (CSF) managers GS-9 and above.*

Fully in accord with the fundamental requirements of the law, this list is confined to documents concerning federal-privilege-connected activities.

(We've already examined the meaning of "employer" elsewhere. I hope the reader will forgive my not going into the lengthy details of the law regarding the specialized and license-dependent subtitle D excise taxes to which Forms 720 and 2290 relate; or those involved with the nature of a U.S. Partnership (except to mention that it is defined as *"two or more persons who join to carry on a trade or business..."*), because I'm not going to do so. However, even those who won't be so generous should find the point of this citation sufficiently established by the fact that the manual instruction does not attempt to claim authority for the production and subscription of a "substitute" 1040 by the Secretary or his delegate.)

This polar opposite legal relationship between the state and federally privileged persons, as compared to that it has with private citizens, is underscored by other provisions within the law. One is a mechanism by which the federal government can recover what it may claim to be owing from such a government-connected party. Recall the language of the authority to levy at which we looked in 'Lies, Damned Lies, And W-2's':

> *Levy may be made upon the accrued salary or wages of any officer, employee, or elected official, of the United States, the District of Columbia, or any agency or instrumentality of the United States or the District of Columbia, by serving a notice of levy on the employer (as defined in section 3401(d)) of such officer, employee, or elected official.*

There is no corresponding authority to seize property from private citizens by mere "notice" to be found within the law.

*****

The 1040 has another purpose-- it is the form specified in the relevant regulations for the making of a claim for refund of amounts improperly withheld.

> *"Even if you do not otherwise have to file a return, you should file one to get a refund of any Federal income tax withheld."*
>
> From the instructions for the 2002 Form 1040

I'll let the relevant code and regulation sections begin the explanation of this aspect of the law:

> *Sec. 6402. - Authority to make credits or refunds*
>
> *(a) General rule*
>
> *In the case of any overpayment, the Secretary, within the applicable period of limitations, may credit the amount of such overpayment, including any interest allowed thereon, against any liability in respect of an internal revenue tax on the part of the person who made the overpayment and shall, subject to subsections (c), (d), and (e)* [deductions for past due obligations to federal or state agencies -PH] *refund any balance to such person.*

> *Sec. 301.6402-3 Special rules applicable to income tax.*
>
> *(a) In the case of a claim for credit or refund filed after June 30, 1976--*
>
> > *(1) In general, in the case of an overpayment of income taxes, a claim for credit or refund of such overpayment shall be made on the appropriate income tax return.*
> >
> > *...*
> >
> > *(5) A properly executed individual, fiduciary, or corporation original income tax return or an amended return (on 1040X or 1120X if applicable) shall constitute a claim for refund or*

> *credit within the meaning of section 6402 and section 6511 for the amount of the overpayment disclosed by such return (or amended return).*

Even language as seemingly straightforward as that above actually incorporates hidden meanings and complicating elements. To begin with, "overpayment" is itself a custom-defined legal term within the law:

> *"The term "overpayment" includes that part of the amount of the payment of any internal revenue tax which is assessed or collected after the expiration of the period of limitation properly applicable thereto."*

and would not, on its face, apply to the circumstances of non-"taxpayers". Indeed, until the enactment of the Current Tax Payment Act of 1943, the law made no particularly explicit provisions for dealing with the refund of amounts taken from persons for whom no tax liability existed. But with that act, doubtless in recognition of the fact that its easily misunderstood language could lead to withholding being improperly applied to non-government persons, Congress added the sections establishing penalties for fraudulent or erroneous W-2's at which we looked in 'Lies, Damned Lies, and W-2's', and amended the existing section relating to the credit for tax withheld on "wages" (section 35), into what are now sections 6401(b)(1) and (c), and 31(a)(1), of the IRC:

> *Section 6401- Amounts treated as overpayments*
>
> *(b) Excessive credits*
>
> *(1) In general*
>
> *If the amount allowable as credits under subpart C of part IV of subchapter A of chapter 1 (relating to refundable credits) exceeds the tax imposed by subtitle A (reduced by the credits allowable under subparts A, B, D, and G of such part IV), the*

amount of such excess shall be considered an overpayment.

(c) Rule where no tax liability

An amount paid as tax shall not be considered not to constitute an overpayment solely by reason of the fact that there was no tax liability in respect of which such amount was paid.

(*"Subpart C of part IV of subchapter A of chapter 1"*, to which 6401(b)(1) refers, is:

Sec. 31 -Tax withheld on wages

(a) Wage withholding for income tax purposes

(1) In general

The amount withheld as tax under chapter 24 shall be allowed to the recipient of the income as a credit against the tax imposed by this subtitle.)

You can see that Congress was trying hard to make this simple. This section establishes that amounts withheld under the provisions of Chapter 24 ("employment" withholding) are claimable as overpayments-- even when the amounts were withheld from someone with no associated tax liability, which is to say, a non-"taxpayer". 6401 also precludes the barring of amounts withheld as tax under Chapter 21 (FICA taxes) from being treated as overpayments.

*****

Obviously, anyone who has not received "income" and is being lawfully dealt with by payers will have no need to use a 1040 for the claim of a refund, as nothing will have been withheld in the first place. However, with so many companies co-opted into the scheme, most are not so fortunate. A bit of attention to the simple mechanics of claiming a refund of money erroneously withheld, and responding to incorrect assertions of "income" paid, is therefore in order.

For the record, though it should be fairly obvious, I'm not a CPA or a tax attorney. (If I were, I'd not be very likely to make public the information in this book and kill off my own good thing, would I?) Consequently, I can only describe what I and my wife have done in this regard-- the reader is welcome to do exactly the same, but should not consider themselves to be being advised or encouraged to do so. It is possible that consultation with an honest and well-informed specialist in this field will reveal more appropriate methods for any particular reader, or considerations suggesting the virtues of an alternative approach. Any election to forego that possibility is the reader's responsibility.

In addition to filing a claim for refund on the appropriate form, it is necessary to rebut any erroneous allegations of "income" paid which have been submitted by others, such as those complicit businesses mentioned above. Happily, in addition to the statutory provisions for filing claims at which we have just looked, there are two convenient regulatory provisions which simplify the process of making such corrections.

In the case of contractor payees, the chief evidentiary instrument to be rebutted is the Form 1099. This typically would only need to be done proactively if money has been withheld in connection with the form, and a claim for refund is being made. Otherwise, a 1099 would normally only need to be addressed reactively, in response to an erroneous allegation of "income" receipts filed by a payer upon which the IRS is relying in demanding a tax.

I've included a reproduction of the 2002 version of the form in the appendix for reference. The form itself contains its own corrective mechanism. At the center top is a checkbox by which is indicated that a particular copy is submitted in order to correct erroneous data included on the originals, which have typically been sent to the victim of the error and the IRS.

A payee need merely check this box on the form, make appropriate corrections to the data, and submit the form with a correspondingly accurate tax return. This is how the procedure is described in the "*2002 General Instructions for Forms 1099, 1098, 5498 and W-2G*":

> *2. Incorrect money amount(s), incorrect address, or a return was filed when one should not have been filed. This error requires only one return to make the correction. A. Form 1098, 1099, 5498, or W-2G: 1. Prepare a new information return. 2. Enter an "X" in the "CORRECTED" box (and date (optional)) at the top of the form. 3. Enter the payer, recipient, and account number information exactly as it appeared on the original incorrect return; however, enter all correct money amounts in the correct boxes as they should have appeared on the original return, and enter the recipient's correct address.*

I think it important to also mark a "correcting" Form 1099 with a sworn declaration to the effect that, *"No payments were received by the party identified hereon as "the recipient" from the party identified hereon as "the payer" which were connected with the performance of the functions of a public office, or otherwise constituted gains, profit or income within the meaning of relevant law"*, or whatever else is actually the case.

For dealing with incorrect W-2's, the IRS publishes Form 4852- 'Substitute for Form W-2, or Form 1099R'. A sample 4852 is also in the appendix. The name of the form sufficiently explains its purpose, which is also more-or-less expressed by the instructions on the back of the form:

> *Purpose of Form - Form 4852 is completed by taxpayers or their representatives when their employer gives them an incorrect Form W-2 or an incorrect Form 1099-R.*

> *This form is also used when the employer or payer does not give the taxpayer a Form W-2 or Form 1099-R. This form serves as a substitute for Form W-2, W-2c, or 1099-R. Use this form to file your income tax return.*

Those wanting to use the 4852 should not be put off by the reference in these instructions to "employer" and "taxpayer"-- there is nothing about "taxpayers" on the form itself, and where "employer" appears, 'or payer' immediately follows. The instructions on the back, which were only added to the form in 1998, seem calculated to discourage its use by non-"taxpayers", and I suspect they were added for no other purpose. Look at line 4 as an example. The instruction for line 4 on the back says:

> *"4. Enter the year the taxpayer had taxable income from which Federal taxes were withheld and Form W-2 and/ or Form 1099-R statements were not received."*

This might lead one to believe that in filling in line 4 one would be declaring that one was a "taxpayer" and had "taxable income" for the year marked. However, the actual line instruction on the face of the form says:

> *"4. Please fill in the year at the end of the statement. I have been unable to obtain (or have received an incorrect) Form W-2, Wage and Tax Statement, or Form 1099-R, Distributions From Pensions, Annuities, Retirement or Profit-sharing Plans IRA's, Insurance Contracts, etc., from my employer or payer named below. I have notified the Internal Revenue Service of this fact. The amounts shown below are my best estimates of all wages or payments paid to me and Federal taxes withheld by this employer or payer during ________."*

When the form is signed, what is being attested to is what the face instructions say, not what is implied by the superfluous and misleading versions on the back.

While we're on the subject of line 4, by the way, whenever I have filled out a 4852, I have modified the *"I have notified the Internal Revenue Service of this fact."* by striking *"have notified"* and substituting *"hereby notify".*

The form is, as I noted earlier, easy to complete, particularly when the erroneous W-2 which is being corrected is handy. Almost everything from the faulty form is simply transcribed to the corresponding spot on the 4852-- the only items that change are the amounts of "wages as defined in section 3401(a)" and "wages as defined in section 3121(a)". Where line 8 asks how the amounts in item 7 were arrived at, that same original W-2 provides the answer, as in, "records provided by the payer listed on line 5". Line 9's question about efforts to obtain a corrected W-2 from the payer is answered with whatever is appropriate, which may well be "none".

The instructions provided with a 1040 for the relevant line say:

> *Line 7 Wages, Salaries, Tips, etc.*
> *Enter the total of your wages, salaries, tips, etc. If a joint return, also include your spouse's income. For most people, the amount to enter on this line should be shown in box 1 of their Form(s) W-2.*

Box 1 on a conventional W-2 corresponds to line 7(A)(a) on a Form 4852. The amount found there on the completed 4852(s) is what gets transcribed onto line 7 of the 1040. The rest of the return is completed with similarly scrupulous attention to accuracy, including the *"Federal Income tax withheld from Forms W-2 and 1099"* line, which is the total of lines 7(A)(f), (i) and (j). Remember, FICA taxes are federal "income" taxes, just like any others.

*****

So, what will the IRS do about a claim for refund of amounts withheld from non-"income"?

Most of the time, the agency will just quietly obey a properly-made claim. Occasionally, it will scream and shout, and cry and moan. It might even threaten and harass. But one thing it will *not* do is execute a substitute for a properly prepared and submitted individual return which alleges more "income" than the citizen has acknowledged. No one in the IRS has any personal or direct knowledge regarding such matters.

If it chooses to behave badly in regard to a claim, the agency will generally attempt to deny that the claim exists-- either by declaring that a return was never sent, or by alleging a defect such as to allow the return to be treated as a legal nullity. These pretenses will occasion a "proposed tax", calculated in the most unfavorable way possible, based on the "income" allegations that have been rebutted by the "missing" return. The proposal will invite the target to agree to the agency's view of things with a signature and thereby avoid a threatened accumulation of interest and penalties. As long as the citizen has accurately completed and executed the original return, of course, this is an empty gesture-- just one of several scare tactics that will be deployed in an effort to induce an abandonment of the law and a return to harness.

This brings up the issue of comprehensive witnessing of mailings, by the way. One DOES want to be able to substantiate one's submissions of forms, returns, and responses to the agency; rumor has it that they WILL conveniently lose things one has sent that are troublesome if one doesn't take precautions. All that is necessary is easy enough, though: One simply has a friend who is not a co-signer on the document in question read one's submission, put it in the envelope, and convey it to the postal clerk or UPS guy, etc.. One should never touch it once it has been read by one's friend; and mailings should always be certified with a return-receipt requested.

The agency will also attempt two other significant intimidations. One is to allege that the return in question is "frivolous"-- a violation of section 6702:

Sec. 6702. - Frivolous income tax return

(a) Civil penalty

If -

(1)

any individual files what purports to be a return of the tax imposed by subtitle A but which -

(A)

does not contain information on which the substantial correctness of the self-assessment may be judged, or

(B)

contains information that on its face indicates that the self-assessment is substantially incorrect; and

(2)

the conduct referred to in paragraph (1) is due to -

(A)

a position which is frivolous, or

(B)

a desire (which appears on the purported return) to delay or impede the administration of Federal income tax laws, then such individual shall pay a penalty of $500.

(b) Penalty in addition to other penalties

The penalty imposed by subsection (a) shall be in addition to any other penalty provided by law

This is done in an effort to take advantage of a misunderstanding of the meaning of assessment (as well as to support a contention that no processable return was ever filed). As noted earlier in our discussion of section 6201, assessment is the application of the rate of tax to a previously established taxable figure. Assessment determines the *amount of tax*, not the *amount being taxed.*

> **Assess**
> *1: to determine the rate or amount of (as a tax)*
> *2 a: to impose (as a tax) according to an established rate*
> *b: to subject to a tax, charge, or levy*
> *Example: each property owner was assessed an additional five dollars*
> Merriam-Webster's Dictionary of Law ©1996.

6702 addresses a return by which the accuracy of *assessment* is compromised, not the accuracy of assertions regarding amounts of "income".

The other significant effort to frighten a citizen into surrender to the lawless scheme is the issuance of a "Notice of Deficiency". This is a more-or-less formal notice proposing a calculation of tax without accounting for the original submission, of a kind with the 'we-say-you-never-filed' scenario. Again this notice will be accompanied by an agreement for the target to sign, accepting the proposal (or, of course, such a target can bow and send in a conventional, lawless return)-- at which point "all will be forgiven". The agency never signs these proposals itself, of course, however much it likes to suggest that it can dictate the "income" figure on which citizens will be taxed. Like the section 6702 allegation, the "Notice of Deficiency" is based upon statutory language which does not authorize contemplation of the amount of "income" in play, only the tax upon whatever the citizen has declared that amount to be:

> *Sec. 6211. - Definition of a deficiency*
> *(a) In general*
> *For purposes of this title in the case of income, estate, and gift taxes imposed by subtitles A and B and excise taxes imposed by chapters 41, 42, 43, and 44 the term "deficiency" means the amount by which the tax imposed by subtitle A or B, or chapter 41, 42, 43, or 44 exceeds the excess of -* [a ridiculously complicated

page-and-a-half formula of bureaucratese for determining the difference between the tax on the return and the properly calculated tax]

It is not necessary to look at the remainder of the statute, because the key is in subsection (a): *"the amount by which* ***the tax*** *imposed by..."*. One who has added incorrectly; erred in multiplying a "taxable income" total by the rate of tax; or picked the wrong field in the handy, pre-calculated table provided with a 1040 might have a deficiency compared to a figure arrived at correctly. But one can't have a "deficiency" just because the IRS doesn't like one's assertion as to what *"the tax"* is being imposed on. Harmoniously, "deficiency" provisions apply solely to "taxpayers"-- that is, those whose receipt of sufficient "income" (or other qualification) has already been established.

*****

Section 6201, the first part of which we looked at earlier, contains a useful subsection if IRS recalcitrance should force anyone into court:

> *(d) Required reasonable verification of information returns*
>
> *In any court proceeding, if a taxpayer asserts a reasonable dispute with respect to any item of income reported on an information return filed with the Secretary under subpart B or C of part III of subchapter A of chapter 61 by a third party ... the Secretary shall have the burden of producing reasonable and probative information concerning such deficiency in addition to such information return.*

("*Subpart B or C of part III of subchapter A of chapter 61*" refers to sections 6041 - 6050S, among which are those we examined in 'Crafting A Trade Or Business Plan' and '"W" Is For Weapon'; and section 6051, which we examined in 'Lies, Damned Lies, And W-2's'; as well as sections 6052- payment of wages in the form of group-term life insurance, and 6053- Reporting of Tips).

This principle finds expression elsewhere in the code, as well:

Sec. 7491. - Burden of proof

(a) Burden shifts where taxpayer produces credible evidence

(1) General rule

If, in any court proceeding, a taxpayer introduces credible evidence with respect to any factual issue relevant to ascertaining the liability of the taxpayer for any tax imposed by subtitle A or B, the Secretary shall have the burden of proof with respect to such issue.

Any 'proceeding' involving a non-"taxpayer" will have that status (as opposed to "taxpayer" status) at its heart, in the form of conflicting assertions regarding the nature of his or her earnings. For as long as that contest is sustained, a non-"taxpayer" can take advantage of these provisions (having appropriately stipulated that no admissions are being made thereby) while neutralizing or defeating the factual allegations supporting the argument against them. With the graceful symmetry of judo, once these provisions are no longer available, it is because they are also no longer needed.

Ok, that's how it all works.

Now, go forth and uphold the law!

*****

"Let the jury consider their verdict," the King said, for about the twentieth time that day.
"No, no!" said the Queen. "Sentence first-- verdict afterwards."
"Stuff and nonsense!" said Alice loudly. "The idea of having the sentence first!"
"Hold your tongue!" said the Queen, turning purple.
"I won't!" said Alice.
"Off with her head!" the Queen shouted at the top of her voice. Nobody moved.
"Who cares for you?" said Alice (she had grown to her full size by this time). "You're nothing but a pack of cards!"

Part Three

(The Nature Of The Crisis)

Good intentions will always be pleaded for any assumption of power. The Constitution was made to guard the people against the dangers of good intentions. There are men in all ages who mean to govern well, but they mean to govern. They promise to be good masters, but they mean to be masters.
-Daniel Webster

Necessity is the plea for every infringement of human freedom. It is the argument of tyrants; it is the creed of slaves.
-William Pitt

The evils of tyranny are rarely seen but by him who resists it.
-John Hay

Resistance to tyrants is obedience to God.
-Thomas Jefferson

Why It Matters

There is not and never has been a federal tax on private receipts (or the activities that produce them), and in fact, as recently as the early 1940's, no truly serious attempt to pretend that such a tax existed had ever been made. Nonetheless, such a tax seems to be an integral part of our lives now-- indeed, so ubiquitous as to seem a part of the natural order. This is not because it is or has become legal, inevitable or fit. It is merely because the interest served by the pretense is rapacious and amoral, its beneficiary-- and therefore defensive-- cadre is large and well-positioned, and its victims are immersed in disinformation.

In fact, the "tax's" ubiquity is carefully generated and maintained, for, being illegal and a fraud, its success relies upon a thicket of lies so necessarily comprehensive as to have become background noise in most people's lives. It has been famously observed that a tangled weave is needed to implement a deceit. A racket by which 250 million people are conned every day for nearly the whole of their lives out of an enormous portion of their wealth production requires and inspires a web of such magnitude and pervasiveness as to strongly endanger, if not choke off completely, the very objective cognition needed to perceive its existence.

Indeed, this scheme has ensconced itself so thoroughly in the world-view of many people that they themselves contribute to its density. Partaking of the character of all big, institutionally promoted lies, the private-receipts tax scheme induces in many of its victims a "Stockholm Syndrome" in which those unable to escape an assailant come to terms with their plight through a delusional sublimation of their own interests to those of their victimizer. Such victims construct "facts" as needed to suit the requirements of the delusion, and abandon contrary knowledge. These "facts" add to the numbing and confusing din to which every other target of the scheme is subjected, and promote a lemming-like embrace of what seems to be the general understanding of the truth, or at least the wisest path to follow. This might be described as the practice of irrational ignorance.

As the ranks of such capitulating victims grow, the delusion generates a defensive political energy favoring its object which is broader and more subtle than the simple self-interest of its beneficiaries: The delusion becomes the "common knowledge"-- a part of the worldview of its victims. Any assault on the underlying issue is necessarily burdened by an "everything you know is wrong" character which will be resisted instinctively even by those against whose interests it works.

Accordingly, the scheme-- cloaked thoroughly and subversively in a mantle of fear, confusion and legal chicanery-- is now, at best, a Procrustean fiction in obeisance to which all contradictory truths must be distorted. The harm it does is fundamental and growing, and as long as it is allowed to continue no other matter of public policy merits consideration. That last is, of course, an extreme statement, and one which might be made by anyone regarding the particular subject of their focus, but consider the following:

• The implementation and defense of this scheme has required and involved the corrosion of the rule of law in general, and of the integrity of our individual rights and the related Constitutional limits on government power in particular. In service to this voracious monster, the courts, all the way up to the Supreme Court, have let stand uncorrected (and occasionally participated in) corrupt administrations of 'law' effectively gutting the Fourth Amendment protection against general warrants; the Fifth Amendment protections against being forced to provide evidence against oneself and of due process before a loss of property; and the Seventh Amendment guarantee of a jury trial in civil cases. Not the least of this class of offense has been the institutional characterization of punishments of ruinous proportion, in response to alleged "crimes of omission" in which the government claims to be the aggrieved party, as "civil" penalties-- in order that Sixth Amendment protections of a trial by jury for the accused can be circumvented.

The scheme has subverted the guarantee of an independent judiciary by tricking or hounding private citizens into "administrative courts" and has fostered the corrupt practice of congressional delegation of legislative authority to executive branch bureaucrats. All of this and more to defend a scheme so ungainly in its attempt to be what it is not as to cost 65 cents in compliance and collection expenses for every dollar collected (see 'Unhappy Returns', James Payne, Lytton Research & Analysis, 1992).

The beneficiaries of the scheme, in order to defend the extension of the "income" tax from what is lawful to what is lusted after, have been a vigorous force behind recasting the Constitution as a 'living document' (which is to say a malleable tool of demagoguery and craft) susceptible to perversion in all its parts. Once the manipulation or redefinition of any Constitutional language is allowed to stand, all the law becomes what the re-definers say it is, and anything goes. Among the ill effects of this process is the raising of generations of cynical and nihilistic citizens, taught in childhood of our great founding principles but growing up in a through-the-looking-glass reality which puts the lie to them all.

• The tax, as fraudulently administered and defended, is a defiance of federalism and a subversion of sovereignty. The original Articles of Confederation provided no power of taxation to the federal government, because such a power was perceived as dangerous to liberty, in part under the principle that the more distant the taxing power from the citizen, the less responsive it would be to his oversight and discipline. In reluctantly granting a taxing power in the reformed Constitution, specific limitations were placed upon the two forms permitted in order to ensure that the people would retain the ability to restrain a spendthrift congress and exercise their ultimate sovereignty. Specific limitations were also placed upon the objects for which taxes could be sought. As Supreme Court Justice Joseph Story observes in his 1833 Commentaries on the Constitution:

> *§ 904. Before proceeding to consider the nature and extent of the power conferred by this clause, and the reasons, on which it is founded, it seems necessary to settle the grammatical construction of the clause, and to ascertain its true reading. Do the words, "to lay and collect taxes, duties, imposts, and excises," constitute a distinct, substantial power; and the words, "to pay debts and provide for the common defence, and general welfare of the United States," constitute another distinct and substantial power? Or are the latter words connected with the former, so as to constitute a qualification upon them? This has been a topic of political controversy; and has furnished abundant materials for popular declamation and alarm. If the former be the true interpretation, then it is obvious, that under colour of the generality of the words to "provide for the common defence and general welfare," the*

government of the United States is, in reality, a government of general and unlimited powers, notwithstanding the subsequent enumeration of specific powers; if the latter be the true construction, then the power of taxation only is given by the clause, and it is limited to objects of a national character, "for the common defence and the general welfare."

§ 905. The former opinion has been maintained by some minds of great ingenuity, and liberality of views. The latter has been the generally received sense of the nation, and seems supported by reasoning at once solid and impregnable. The reading, therefore, which will be maintained in these commentaries, is that, which makes the latter words a qualification of the former; and this will be best illustrated by supplying the words, which are necessarily to be understood in this interpretation. They will then stand thus: "The congress shall have power to lay and collect taxes, duties, imposts, and excises, in order to pay the debts, and to provide for the common defence and general welfare of the United States;" that is, for the purpose of paying the public debts, and providing for the common defence and general welfare of the United States. In this sense, congress has not an unlimited power of taxation; but it is limited to specific objects,--the payment of the public debts, and providing for the common defence and general welfare. A tax, therefore, laid by congress for neither of these objects, would be unconstitutional, as an excess of its legislative authority. In what manner this is to be ascertained, or decided, will be considered hereafter. At present, the interpretation of the words only is before us; and the reasoning, by which that already suggested has been vindicated, will now be reviewed.

Justice Story proceeds to a simple, straightforward and impeccably logical argument establishing the accuracy of his analysis (which can be found online at http://www.constitution.org/js/js_314.htm).

These elements work together, politically and practically, to discipline the state. The mechanism of Constitutional direct taxation requires-- in the form of an individual, positive act of Congress and the executive-- an identification of the subject of the tax, the purpose of the expenditure, and the specific amount proposed to be collected; while indirect taxes are for the most part avoidable at the will of the citizenry. From the birth of the nation until 1943 this disciplined system proved itself the goose that lays the golden eggs by nurturing the laissez-faire economy that not only stood on its own merits as the only truly moral system, but grew to become one of the greatest benefactors of humanity known to history. American freedom, unburdened as it was by an interfering and confiscatory government, unleashed a productive and innovative genius that uplifted the world. Since then, the antithesis of discipline has taken control.

In effectively imposing, through corrupt and fraudulent administration, an unlimited, unapportioned direct tax on property, the "income" tax scheme has opened a spigot of money into the federal treasury, for no specific purposes, in no specific amount, and by a process all but unavoidable by the "tax" payer. The intended restraint is nullified, and the individual authority of any single citizen is drowned in an ocean of the commons, left with only the thin reed of one vote among 200 million with which to try to turn out the spendthrifts.

Consequently,

• The fraudulent "income" tax scheme is the mother of the activist state. While many programs partake of, and contribute to, the legal and philosophical corruption mentioned earlier, it is the easy money provided by the "income" tax scheme that feeds them all. Government in the United States spent more money (in inflation adjusted dollars) in 2001 alone than it did in the 114 years from 1787 to 1900 *combined* (Stephen Moore, Institute for Policy Innovation report #161, 2002). Not only was this money spent indiscriminately and with abandon, but most of the spending was actively harmful to the interests of those from whom it was taken. Without undertaking to assess particular programs, I will declare it axiomatic that as the amount of money available for government redistribution rises so too does the political servicing of special, narrow interests in defiance of, and therefore to the detriment of, the general market forces upon which we all rely for accurate, reliable information and a level playing field on which to compete. With government at all levels controlling about 50% of the American GDP through taxation (roughly 60% of which proportion is taken through the "income" tax scheme), such occasions are myriad.

This is real "supply-side" economics. An incoming supply of money-- with which constituents can be bribed, patronage financed, and power-bases expanded-- creates a demand for programs by which it can be justified (and every "program" once established becomes a supply of justification, beneficiary constituents, and campaign cash).

At one time, particularly during the first century of the nation's existence when Constitutional direct tax submissions addressed most federal revenue needs other than the extremely insignificant routine operational budget (financed mostly through tariffs), a special expenditure requirement led to the (usually temporary) establishment of a particular revenue stream. Since the successful implementation of the current withholding scheme during the emotional and distracted years of the second world war, the process has been reversed, with the existence of the revenue stream leading to the adoption of special expenditures and the maintenance of old ones whose raison d'etre has long passed. The federal revenue process has thus gone from being a budget to being a sort of a defined-benefit plan, with benefit growth more-or-less matching the steady growth of the revenue stream.

And it *is* steady, and inevitably so; the nature of the scheme ensures this. In times of economic contraction, the federal "income" tax revenue is protected by "bracket creep". This is the pushing of a given amount of wealth-production, such as a worker's annual output, into a higher "tax" bracket (seizure of a larger percentage of the wealth) as the number of dollars needed to represent (and compensate for) that output increases due to the inflation. The activating inflation (expansion of the money supply in excess of the rate of economic expansion) is an inevitable characteristic of contraction-- and is itself a guarantor of the continuity of the federal revenue. Inflation, after all, is nothing more than the injection into the money supply of unaccounted for-- in other words, free-- currency by way of government spending. As such, it represents an economic gain to the government exactly proportional to the devaluation of the public supply of currency. (It may, by the way, be more accurate to say that recession is an inevitable characteristic of inflation, rather than the other way around, but that is a subject for another book).

During economic expansion, the scheme provides for a similar and even more aggressive growth phenomenon in the federal revenue process-- because the revenue arising from a general tax on all economic activity (to which the scheme, in practice, amounts) automatically increases with growth in the economy. Every new business, every new worker, every new market and every productivity boost represents an increase in the scheme's "tax base". This is why the federal budget has held basically steady as a percentage of the economy since the dedicated implementation of the "income" tax scheme in the mid 1940's despite the relative explosion of personal wealth and general productivity improvements during the same period, both of which should have diminished the government share of the economy.

In the real world, of course, the kid who cuts your grass doesn't get an automatic and proportional increase in his price per acre as your wealth increases; rather his price, in real dollars, stays about the same-- and diminishes as a percentage of your increasing wealth. A legitimate, need-based (demand-driven) federal budget is subject to the same simple economic principles. Only in the looking-glass world of the "income" tax scheme can the federal revenue have become a cancerous organic component of the general economy, sharing the larger organism's growth rate in good times and exceeding it in bad.

In the end, the only aspect of the current federal revenue process still reminiscent of budgeting is the occasional tax-rate (or object) fine-tuning which is undertaken to shift attention away from some particular boondoggle that has errantly caught the public eye. This is not actual budgeting, of course, it's just smoke-and-mirror politicking. Overall, the level of spending just continues to go nowhere but up, year after year.

• The scheme, as fraudulently administered and defended, is inherently divisive. When control of 50% of the nation's wealth production is in play, the individual interests of everyone are also at stake; therefore, influencing that control becomes the natural imperative of all citizens with the requisite capacity of either wealth or numbers-- and the shameful victimization of all those without.

Thus, in asserting broad and inescapable claims, the "income" tax scheme induces in the community the arbitrary, degenerate and brutal *"war of all against all"* that darkened Thomas Hobbes's narrow, but celebrated, vision of human relations-- and against which the Founders provided, through careful and deliberate limitations on the powers and purposes of their creations. Hobbes, perceiving that a power vacuum results in anarchy and chaos, but not fully understanding the dynamics of individual self-interest, and not guided by respect for individual rights, saw no alternative but a centralization of power-- a view embraced and promoted then and now by anyone who wishes to exercise power over others.

It was the Founders' superior understanding that any centralization of significant power simply institutionalizes and makes constant the abuse of some by others, producing steady-state oppression punctuated by periodic struggles for supremacy in the all-or-nothing relationship. They also recognized that this was true not only of an autocracy or oligarchy but also of the alternative of an unrestricted democracy, which inevitably devolves into a self-eviscerating despotism as a majority learns that it can command power to its benefit at the inescapable expense of a victimized minority. As James Madison observed,

> *"Democracies have been found incompatible with personal security or the rights of property; and in general been as short in their lives as they have been violent in their death."*

Their deep comprehension of, and reverence for, the principles of sovereignty and natural law led these brilliant men unerringly to the true solution: The institutional acknowledgement that power originates in each individual citizen. This diffuse power-- accompanied by a fluid civil mechanism with which it can be coordinated at need, but dependent on the voluntary, self-interested cooperation of its disparate elements-- uniquely minimizes the incentive for ruinous and bitter struggles for its control, provides sufficient security for participants, and ensures that abuse and oppression at its hands would be only isolated, occasional and brief. (Though it may offend the socialist sensibility, no small part of the benefits of this solution are in its providing the best assurances that the wise and prudent might avoid, or at least survive, the ill effects of the infatuations and mis-directions of the foolish, however common foolishness might become).

Today, the centralization of control over half the productivity of the nation through the "income" tax scheme undoes all these benefits of the Founder's genius. Commanding the labor of the population by seizure of its fungible fruits, the state thereby exercises more dominion over Americans than was suffered by medieval serfs at the hands of their feudal lords; and the micromanagement of their lives financed by (and, incredibly, used as a justification for) much of that pelf has no parallel outside of the most despotic of totalitarian experiments. The struggle to control this enormous power-- against which no one is secure and which is inherently abusive and oppressive-- has become the national pastime, incidentally corrupting even the simplest and most fundamental elements of the political process. Political philosopher P. J. O'Rourke has concisely summarized the general character of this effect in observing,

> *"When buying and selling are controlled by Washington, the first things to be bought and sold are politicians".*

• The nature of the fraudulent tax scheme impels its beneficiaries to encourage (and, insofar as it is within their power, to produce) an ignorant population. A great historical ignorance is necessary to permit the embrace, for example, of the government-promoted myth that in 1913 (when the 16th Amendment was passed) the ascendant and muscular populist movement fastened upon the country a tax reaching all economic transactions-- including the recompense from long hours of labor received by the common workers of which it was predominantly composed. That such a thing would be proposed by any political majority is unlikely at best; that it should have been done by this particularly class-conscious movement, nurtured as it was by a conviction that fat-cat robber-barons controlled the federal government-- including the application of its taxing powers-- is absurd.

Comparably ludicrous is the attendant implication that the drafters of such a self-inflicted wound must simply have failed to recognize the need to repeal (or at least modify) Article 1, Section 9, despite their amendment's being a response to a

73-page Supreme Court opinion which dwelt often and at length on just that portion of the Constitution. The truth, of course, is that the drafters did not recognize such a need because there was no need. The 16th Amendment had no purpose beyond establishing that the robber-baron contingent of government contract-holders, lease-holders, license-holders and bond-holders-- otherwise subject to the existing indirect excise on the "gains, profits and income" resulting from the exercise of such government privileges-- could not shield its federally connected activities from the tax by asserting their association with personal property.

That these myths, and others of the same ilk, are even in circulation, considering the clear words of the Constitution (not to mention the Supreme Court's frequently repeated declarations that, *"The provisions of the Sixteenth Amendment conferred no new power of taxation..."*) is a testament to the abject failure, at the very least, of the government education industry for which we pay so much-- if not its calculated subordination to the interests of the scheme's beneficiaries. All of the corruptions of law, morals, prudence and understanding essential to the "income" tax scheme can only hold sway over a population generally weak in both knowledge and wisdom. It is, therefore, in perfect harmony with the scheme that governments at all levels have complacently or complicitly allowed the public education industry to steadily devolve from its original mission of preparing sovereign citizens for the responsibilities of adulthood into a combination of day-care, vocational training, and laboratory for unproven 'educational' fads.

A recent report on the state of civics education in America today by the National Center for Policy Analysis reflects this degeneration:

> *"According to a survey of top seniors at 55 colleges and universities by the Roper organization:*

- *While nearly 100 percent could identify cartoon characters Beavis and Butthead and rapper Snoop Doggy Dogg, only 34 percent knew George Washington was the American general at the battle of Yorktown.*
- *Only a third were able to identify the Constitution as establishing the division of powers in the U.S. government.*
- *Eighty-one percent of those top students earned a D or F in response to basic historical questions.*

Only 25 states now require any civics education in public schools at all, and U.S. adults finished last in a nine-nation survey asking respondents to identify regions and countries on an unmarked map of the world. Fourteen percent couldn't even find the United States."

Analyzing the 1998 National Assessment of Educational Proficiency, wakingbear.com observes that,

> *"The NAEP test showed that 35% of America's high school seniors didn't even have an understanding of civics that experts consider "basic." Another 39% only scored at the basic level. Just 22% of seniors had a "proficient" understanding of how the American government works. And one in 25 scored at the "advanced" level.*
>
> *Results for the other grades tested - 4th and 8th - mirrored those of the high-school seniors, with less than one in four students scoring at or above the level deemed "proficient." And a closer look at high-school seniors' responses to individual questions often suggests they do not know why American government is set up the way it is. For example, just one in four seniors could come up with two ways the U.S. system of government prevents the exercise of "absolute arbitrary*

power" on the part of the government. Among the 14 possible answers were such basics as the Bill of Rights, an independent judiciary, civilian control of the military - and the right to vote.

On a multiple-choice question asking the purpose of the Bill of Rights, one-third of high school seniors did not know that it was written to limit the power of the federal government. Not one in 10 seniors could identify two ways that a democracy benefits from the active participation of its citizens. Just over a third knew that the Supreme Court pointed to the Constitution's 14th Amendment when it began to overturn segregation laws.

That shouldn't come as much of a surprise. Other surveys, both formal and informal, suggest that America's future voters and jurors simply do not know much about the country's founding.

In a 1998 poll conducted by the National Constitution Center, not one in 50 American teenagers could identify James Madison as the father of the U.S. Constitution. Not even half could name the three branches of the federal government. And not one in ten could name the landmark Supreme Court case (Brown vs. Board of Education) that ended segregation in the public schools. And in an informal survey of Bay area teenagers, San Francisco Examiner reporter Emily Gurnon found that less than half of the 4 dozen teens she quizzed could name the country from which the U.S. won its independence.

Gurnon asked what July 4th celebrated. One high-school graduate told her, "It's like the freedom. Some war was fought and we won, so we got our freedom." From which country? That graduate didn't know.

> *Another high school graduate also knew that July 4th celebrated America's independence. From which country? "I want to say Korea," he told Gurnon. How long ago did it take place? "Like 50 years," he guessed."*

The rapid spread of government schooling during the 20th century was, undoubtedly, innocently coincidental with the concurrent implementation of the "income" tax scheme. Similarly, the de-emphasis of history, logic, and meaningful "civics" in those schools over the last forty years probably serves, and is primarily responsive to, other interests. Although it would be too much to blame the uninterrupted decline of quality in public schools and their curricula on the scheme, still, that decline has unquestionably contributed to its success. Applying the principle of 'cui bono', it is reasonable to conclude that the governments which control the public schools have been operating under a powerful incentive to simply let them continue to fail. Thus, this pernicious fraud manages not only to darken our own minds and lives, but to blight those of our children as well.

• Effectively presented as an involuntary requirement, the scheme corrupts our fundamental principle of equal treatment under the law with a progressive structure under which some citizens are able to force a benefit for themselves out of the pockets of their neighbors. This callous design, intended to maximize the protective political support for the scheme by invoking Shaw's principle that, *"A government which robs Peter to pay Paul can always depend on the support of Paul"*, engenders institutional endorsement of the proposition that a form of slavery is a fundamental element of social justice. (Where the tax lawfully applies, of course-- as an expected cost of voluntarily enjoying the benefit of federal privilege-- unequal treatment is no more unfair than is having to pay more for good seats at the show).

This is a particularly noxious perversion, in that under this "justice" a heavier burden is extracted from some Americans precisely because they have *already* made a greater contribution to the common weal than others. After all, one earns one's *unprivileged* receipts solely by serving the interests of one's neighbors.

Furthermore, contrary to the many false intellections marshaled to support this aspect of the scheme, the more such receipts that one's good service brings in, the *less* demand one places on, and the *less* benefit one has from the community resources-- making the progressive structure of the tax even more obscene. The reality is that a successful wealth-producer has typically been more adamant and persistent than others in *defying* and surmounting the public infrastructure and its typically sclerotic defense of the status quo. (The exception is those who have used government to their advantage; their gains, of course, *are* the lawful objects of the "income" tax as properly applied).

As to public services, the well-to-do place far less demand on such expenses than others-- they draw no public welfare, they are privately insured, they live where the local services are equitably paid for out of (typically) high local tax rates. In other words, they pay their own way. The vigorous efforts of many in positions of authority and respect to seduce Americans into accepting the standing of these truths on their heads, in order to ensure that the gravy-train of professional fees, bureaucratic power, and re-election will continue, is a national scandal. That these efforts have largely been successful is a national shame.

Finale

Our Constitutionally prescribed system of federal taxation partakes of the fundamental moral and legal principle that each person is the exclusive owner of his or her own body, labor, and judgment-- a principle so unfailingly sound and self-evident that every human being that ever lived has claimed its protection, at least for themselves. It is among the key mechanisms making possible one of the greatest achievements in human history: The truly practical and, overall, harmonious organization of a large and widely-dispersed society providing security, economic vitality, resources and room, by virtue of which the rights of Americans were well secured for many, many years even as the nation rose to ever-greater general prosperity despite periodic wars, recessions, and social upheavals. Such an organization is naturally and necessarily dependent for its success and stability (not to mention its worth) upon scrupulous respect for property rights, along with the rule of law.

The restoration and preservation of this blessed and beneficent legacy-- for ourselves, our fellows and our posterity-- is, I believe, among the paramount obligations of American citizenship. The alternative, no matter how persuasively promoted or defended, is one form or another of illegitimate and despicable tyranny. Each and every such alternative amounts to no more and no less than the coerced subordination of the interests of the less powerful to the appetites of the militarily or politically stronger-- the degree of victimization within any of which is limited only by temporary forbearance of the dominant or the vagaries of fortune.

However restrained any system admitting of a forcible claim by others to the property or labor of their neighbor might be at any particular time, at its very best it must be hobbled by uncertainty and constant struggle. Inevitably, of course, such despotisms ultimately degenerate into naked slavery. After all, by what argument can the claim to more be denied when the claim to a little has been acknowledged? And is it not the nature of man to lower the bar steadily, once it has been let move at all? To say otherwise is to be naïve or disingenuous, and in defiance of all the lessons of history.

The "income" tax scheme and much of the juggernaut of government that it sustains manifestly stand as deep-rooted impediments to the fulfillment of our civic responsibility. It is fortunate, therefore, that however obscure and misunderstood they may have become, the actual statutes relating to taxation have remained consistent with, and respectful of, the wise and critical requirements laid down by the founders in the fundamental law. All that each of us need do is invoke the written law and claim the return of money improperly withheld; de-authorize improper withholdings for the future; rebut any erroneous assertions by others who have paid us; correct any improper assertions that we have made ourselves... while being ready to abide the storm of protest, denial, resistance, threats, intimidation and perhaps injustice which might follow.

Not too long ago, those filing correctly prepared 1040's would simply get a check in the mail or be met with the silent acceptance of their submissions, whichever was appropriate. This was so even of some types of filings prepared without comprehensive knowledge of the law, but done solely in light of core Constitutional principles and thus having managed to arrive at the legally correct result. The benign responses to these filings were those of a system taking no special notice of them and simply following the rules, in the mindless, automatic fashion to which bureaucracies are prone.

As the volume of educated filings has risen over the years, the deadly threat to the scheme represented by widespread knowledge of the law and how to prepare an accurate return has come to be very much on the mind of its administrator-beneficiaries. These "public servants" have frantically engaged in a variety of efforts to discourage upstanding, educated filers. As I mentioned in 'About 1040's, And Claiming Refunds', most accurate claims result in prompt, law-abiding responses. But such a claim now faces an increasing chance of being met with a deliberate effort to trick or intimidate the filer into withdrawing or compromising the claim and settling back into the expensive and unprincipled but familiar and unthreatening role of obedient, servile member of the hive. We've discussed many of the methods that are used in this effort.

Those who are simply diligent in taking care to declare, attest to, and sign off on no more and no less than what they know to be true cannot be harmed, when all is said and done, by these venal and ever-so-close-to-utterly-lawless efforts. Nonetheless, the defense of the gravy-train which will be mounted by the political class, the bureaucracy, the professional camp-followers, and the other net-tax-beneficiaries will be ferocious until the very last of them have been obliged to find honest work. While the abandonment of ourselves and our children to the humiliation and relative impoverishment of servitude now, and to the barbarism of utter lawlessness in the future, is terrible to contemplate and a powerful motivation to stand up for what is right, taking on entrenched and corrupt opposition is tough and dangerous.

So, what to do?

As luck would have it, I write these words on Independence Day, 2003, with flags waving on every building that I can see through my window, and the routine sounds of the day punctuated constantly by the booms and cracklings of fireworks near and far. It is thus very easy to bring to mind the words of many inspired guides from which any consideration of the proper course might benefit.

Taking full advantage of this fortuitous opportunity, I leave you, dear reader-- with my very best wishes, and my sincerest thanks for the time you have given me-- in the wonderfully capable hands of Patrick Henry. It was not really all that long ago that this great man, and the rest of his remarkable generation of Americans, faced an even greater test of courage and resolve. They had no more to lose by surrender than we do today, but everything to lose, including their lives, by refusing to stand down. Henry spoke for them all when he answered the challenge. This is what he said:

> *They tell us, sir, that we are weak; unable to cope with so formidable an adversary. But when shall we be stronger? Will it be the next week, or the next year? Will it be when we are totally disarmed, and when a British guard shall be stationed in every house? Shall we gather strength by irresolution and inaction? Shall we acquire the means of effectual resistance by lying supinely on our backs and hugging the delusive phantom of hope, until our enemies shall have bound us hand and foot? Sir, we are not weak if we make a proper use of those means which the God of nature hath placed in our power. The millions of people, armed in the holy cause of liberty, and in such*

a country as that which we possess, are invincible by any force which our enemy can send against us. Besides, sir, we shall not fight our battles alone. There is a just God who presides over the destinies of nations, and who will raise up friends to fight our battles for us. The battle, sir, is not to the strong alone; it is to the vigilant, the active, the brave. Besides, sir, we have no election. If we were base enough to desire it, it is now too late to retire from the contest. There is no retreat but in submission and slavery! Our chains are forged! Their clanking may be heard on the plains of Boston! The war is inevitable-- and let it come! I repeat it, sir, let it come.

It is in vain, sir, to extenuate the matter. Gentlemen may cry, Peace, Peace-- but there is no peace. The war is actually begun! The next gale that sweeps from the north will bring to our ears the clash of resounding arms! Our brethren are already in the field! Why stand we here idle? What is it that gentlemen wish? What would they have? Is life so dear, or peace so sweet, as to be purchased at the price of chains and slavery? Forbid it, Almighty God! I know not what course others may take; but as for me, give me liberty or give me death!

***

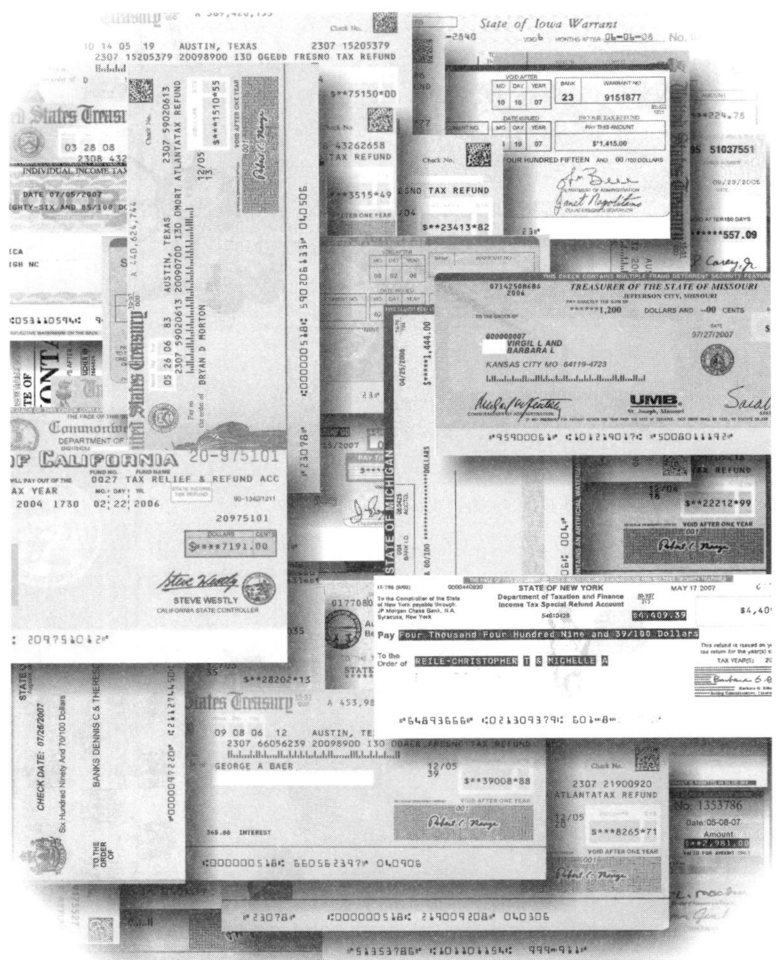
State of Iowa Warrant
AUSTIN, TEXAS
2307 15205379 20098900 130 OGEDD FRESNO TAX REFUND
INDIVIDUAL INCOME TAX
DATE 07/05/2007
2307 59020613
AUSTIN, TEXAS
BRYAN D MORTON
VOID AFTER ONE YEAR
$***1510*55
$**75150*00
TAX REFUND
$**3515*49
FRESNO TAX REFUND
$**23413*82
WARRANT NO
9151877
PAY THIS AMOUNT
$*1,415.00
FOUR HUNDRED FIFTEEN AND 00/100 DOLLARS
**224.78
51037551
*****557.09
TREASURER OF THE STATE OF MISSOURI
JEFFERSON CITY, MISSOURI
******1,200
DOLLARS AND -00 CENTS
07/27/2007
VIRGIL L AND
BARBARA L
KANSAS CITY MO 64119-4723
UMB
$*****1,444.00
STATE OF MICHIGAN
OF CALIFORNIA
0027 TAX RELIEF & REFUND ACC
TAX YEAR
2004 1730 02 22 2006
20975101
$****7191.00
STEVE WESTLY
CALIFORNIA STATE CONTROLLER
TAX REFUND
$**22212*99
VOID AFTER ONE YEAR
STATE OF NEW YORK
Department of Taxation and Finance
Income Tax Special Refund Account
MAY 17 2007
$4,409.39
Pay Four Thousand Four Hundred Nine and 39/100 Dollars
To the Order of REILE-CHRISTOPHER T & MICHELLE A
CHECK DATE: 07/26/2007
Six Hundred Ninety And 70/100 Dollars
BANKS DENNIS C & THERESE
TO THE ORDER OF
$**28202*13
09 08 06 12 AUSTIN, TEXAS
2307 66056239 20098900 130 ODAER FRESNO TAX REFUND
GEORGE A BAER
$**39008*88
VOID AFTER ONE YEAR
365.86 INTEREST
2307 21900920
ATLANTATAX REFUND
$***8265*71
VOID AFTER ONE YEAR
No. 1353786
Date:05-08-07
Amount
$**2,981.00

Appendix

ഇ൨ഇ൨

First, A Pleasant Report

Although this book (CtC) contains several warnings that those who stand up and act in accordance with the real requirements and limitations of the law should be prepared for strenuous and nearly lawless resistance from the government, over the years I have been pleasantly surprised in this regard. Shortly after the book first went to print, I became the first American in history to secure a refund of Social Security and Medicare 'contributions' (along with everything else withheld), when my own federal refund claim for 2002 was properly honored. Since then, thousands of CtC readers across America have risen to uphold the law, and the vast majority have also enjoyed law-abiding responses from both the IRS and dozens of state tax agencies. The amounts recovered have ranged from as little as 78 cents to over $134,000.00 in one refund.

Nonetheless, I do not intend to revoke-- or even modify-- those warnings. Some readers have been targeted by obnoxious tax agency efforts to confuse and discourage claimants. Happily, the number subjected to these efforts is small (and even among this small group it often turns out that the real focus or pretext for the agency attention is some pre-CtC bad practice that resists being undone, or has residual consequences). This tax agency behavior has remained within the law, but it demonstrates a deliberate, if increasingly frantic, government policy of resistance to the inconvenient truth.

In a few cases these efforts have taken the form of the misapplication of the "frivolous return" statute as discussed in 'About 1040s And Claiming Refunds'. A few other readers have been treated to a variety of other, more inventive (if utterly corrupt) efforts to discourage their claims. For instance, some have received a notice declaring an "appealable disallowance of claim" because, "you based your claim on your [erroneous] view that wages and salaries do not constitute taxable income". Of course, nothing could be further from the truth-- readers of 'Cracking the Code-...' are perfectly aware that "wages" are "income", and would never suggest otherwise.

What these claimants have actually asserted, of course, is that their earnings are not "wages"-- quite a different thing altogether. Unable to challenge or dispute such assertions, but unwilling to admit defeat, the government is falling back on the childish pretense that it misunderstands what is being said. In fact, this pretense of misunderstanding and mischaracterization is the foundation for all tax agency efforts to discourage or thwart CtC-educated Americans.

Needless to say, the government's finding it necessary to mischaracterize the claim it wishes to thwart serves to underscore the accuracy of the knowledge upon which that claim is based. It is highly significant, and should be lost on no one, that the government's response is not to simply declare the claimant's earnings to be "wages", or to declare those earnings to be "income" (or simply to declare them taxable, regardless of labels), which it certainly would do if these things were true (or would declare regardless of the truth, if possessed of the power to do so). Although these mischaracterizations are accompanied by a fair bit of bluster, they are devoid of legal substance. (See www.losthorizons.com/tax/RevealingPloys.htm for extended discussion of this subject.)

Indeed, the nature of these government efforts to prop up the scheme in the face of an informed American public simply validates the aptness of my 'Alice In Wonderland' motif. However corrupt the motivation which informs them, these efforts are those of the paper-thin pack of cards which, in the end, Alice disdainfully recognized her tormentors to be.

Still, and again, the most typical governmental response to the filings of those who have studied CtC is a scrupulously proper capitulation to the requirements of the law. The concrete manifestations of these pleasing responses can be enjoyed at www.losthorizons.com/tax/MoreVictories.htm.

*****

A Few Observations About Filling Out Forms

In the vast majority of cases the only difference between filling out tax forms in ignorance of the law and filling them out in knowledge of the law will be the "income" amounts one starts with. (Another, consequent difference is that, in most cases, starting with accurate "income" figures will mean that there ARE no complicated calculations, deductions, etc, to concern oneself with. Educated Americans will typically find themselves doing their taxes in ten minutes, and without boxes of receipts, an adding machine, two packs of cigarettes and a stiff drink afterward to numb the sense of having just bent over for another annual..., well, let's just call it an "indignity"...)

In the most general terms, this means that where a form asks for an original figure (that is, not the mere product of a calculation involving figures already entered thereon), a filer should take care to record what is precisely correct to the best of his or her own fully-educated knowledge and belief, paying careful attention to the fact that every such entry constitutes both a declaration as to an amount, AND a declaration as to the legal character of that amount. Both of these considerations apply to figures transferred from other forms, as well: If the filer transfers such a figure to a form he or she is completing, he or she is declaring that the figure involved is both accurate as to the amount, and to the legal status of that amount.

This is also true of any figures on any form submitted with a return. By such a submission (or transcription), the filer is explicitly endorsing the accuracy-- both as to the amount, and as to the legal character-- of any figures on such a form (or as transcribed). That's why the law provides for, and fully accommodates, a filer replacing inaccurate originals of any forms needing to be attached to a return with accurate instruments reflecting his or her own testimony.

By the way, some will find it useful to bear in mind that when a CPA, or other service-provider "does somebody's taxes", that service-provider operates on the assumption that the customer is deliberately and knowingly certifying the accuracy of everything handed over to him or her in the way of documents and "information returns". For instance, if someone hands over a W-2 (or other "information return") to a tax preparer, the tax-preparer takes that as THE CUSTOMER'S declaration or agreement that everything reported on that form is accurate (and it is the customer who will finalize and take responsibility for that certification by signing the completed return). The service-provider is not making such determinations for himself, nor could he. After all, what does he know about the circumstances reflected on any such form? Precisely the same is true when a service-provider is given a 4852 or other instrument by which the filer is correcting forms known to have been sent to the relevant tax agency with whom the return being prepared will be filed.

The only thing for which such a service-provider is responsible (and the only thing that is his legitimate concern) is the accuracy of his calculations in processing the numbers given to him, and the accuracy of his application of relevant deductions and so forth to, and in connection with, those provided numbers. The filer, and no one but the filer, determines the "income" amounts involved.

*****

Some Interesting History On The Current Withholding Provisions

The following excerpt is taken from the transcript of a withholding tax hearing before a subcommittee of the committee on finance, United States Senate, during the 77th Congress, Second Session on data relative to withholding provisions of the 1942 Revenue Act on August 21 and 22, 1942. The excerpts are of exchanges between Senators John A. Danaher and Bennett Clark and testifying witnesses Charles O. Hardy of the Brookings Institution and Milton Friedman of the Treasury Department Division of Tax Research.

This material originally came to my attention in autumn, 2005, as some of the vast quantity of unsubstantiated flotsam and jetsam with which the internet is awash. However, it was intriguing, so I contacted the National Archives and Records Administration in Washington. Two very helpful and courteous administrative staffers, Rod Ross and Maryellen Trautman, undertook to research it for me, and reported back two interesting things. The first was that the transcript is legitimate. The second was that, while they were able to verify these excerpts, they were unable to provide me with a hard copy of the transcript-- because it is, and has always been, classified. (My correspondents speculate that a copy of the transcript was individually declassified at some point in the past, perhaps for inclusion in the library of one of the hearing participants, and thus was able to find its way into circulation.)

Here is the significant passage:

Senator Clark: *"Of course, you withhold not only from taxpayers but nontaxpayers."*

Mr. Hardy: *"Yes."*

...

Senator Danaher: *"I have only one other thought on that point. In the event of withholding from the owner of stock and no taxes due ultimately, where does he get his refund?"*

Mr. Friedman: *"You're thinking of a corporation or an individual?"*

Senator Danaher: *"I am talking about an individual."*

Mr. Friedman: *"An individual will file an income tax return, and that income tax return will constitute an automatic claim for refund."*

In the end, of course, the withholding provisions that made their way into the law under the Current Tax Withholding Act of 1943 were confined in their application to 'taxpayers' only, as a matter of legal necessity. Nonetheless, provisions acknowledging and addressing the possibility that withholding would, as a practical matter, inevitably end up being misapplied were also thoughtfully included; and the mechanism of the 1040 as the remediating instrument was formally adopted, as is discussed in detail in the chapter 'About 1040s, And Claiming Refunds'.

*****

Regarding The Legal Meaning Of "State" And "Person"

> *"[T]he following propositions may be considered as established:*
>
> ...

3. That the District of Columbia and the territories are states as that word is used in [tax] *treaties with foreign powers, with respect to the ownership, disposition, and inheritance of property;"* United States Supreme Court, Downes v. Bidwell, 182 U.S. 244, (1901).

Per the Revised Statutes, Title XXXV- Internal Revenue, Section 3140 (currently represented by 26 USC 7701(a)(1) and (10), and 26 USC 7651):

"The word "State" when used in this title shall be construed to include the Territories and the District of Columbia, where such construction is necessary to carry out its provisions.

(This usage extends throughout federal law. 42 USC 303, relating to payments to States of old-age assistance grants, serves as a good example:

(a) Computation of amounts

From the sums appropriated therefor, the Secretary of the Treasury shall pay to each State which has a plan approved under this subchapter, for each quarter, beginning with the quarter commencing October 1, 1960—

(1) Repealed. Pub. L. 97–35, title XXI, § 2184(a)(4)(A), Aug. 13, 1981, 95 Stat. 816.

(2) in the case of Puerto Rico, the Virgin Islands, and Guam, an amount equal to one-half of the total of the sums expended during such quarter as old-age assistance under the State plan, not counting so much of any expenditure with respect to any month as exceeds $37.50 multiplied by the total number of recipients of old-age assistance for such month; plus

...)

As for the several states of the Union, on the other hand,

> *"It is unnecessary to lay special stress on the title to the soil in which the channels were dug* [Boston, Massachusetts], *but it may be noticed that it was not in the United States."* United States Supreme Court, Ellis v. United States, 206 U.S. 246; 27 S.Ct. 600 (1907).

> Now, continuing with R. S. 3140:
> *"And where not otherwise distinctly expressed or manifestly incompatible with the intent thereof, the word "person", as used in this title, shall be construed to mean and include a partnership, association, company, or corporation, as well as a natural person."*

The 'code' representation of the definition of "person", which is a consolidation of 10 statutes, leaves out the phrase 'natural person'. The draftsmen relied on the term 'individual' to express the same meaning. Nonetheless, the actual language of R.S. 3140 remains the law. Unfortunately, some theorists-- whose 'research' began and ended with nothing more than the code-- have erroneously concluded that "person" in the law only means some kind of artificial entity. This has led, as might be imagined, to all manner of wild flights of fancy regarding the nature of the "income" tax structure.

> ***Person.*** *In general usage, a human being (i.e. natural person), though by statute term may include a firm, labor organization, partnerships, associations, corporations, legal representatives, trustees, trustees in bankruptcy, or receivers.* Black's Law Dictionary, 5th edition.

> ***Individual.*** *As a noun, this term denotes a single person as distinguished from a group or class, and also, very commonly, a private or natural person as distinguished from a partnership, corporation, or*

> *association; but it is said that this restrictive signification is not necessarily inherent in the word, and that it may, in proper cases, include artificial persons.* Black's Law Dictionary, 2nd Edition

(There ARE places in the law where "person" has a more limited meaning. Such places will furnish a custom definition of the term, and the exclusive range of its application, as in, *"For purposes of this subchapter..."*)

*****

Regarding References In The Law To "Professions, Trades, Employments, Vocations, Etc..."

Occasionally, a provision of law or a judicial ruling will make a reference to "professions, trades, employments, vocations, etc." in connection with the "income" tax, leading the non-CtC-educated to imagine (or contend) that the tax applies to anyone engaging in any profession, trade, occupation, and so forth. This misunderstanding appears to result from a general ignorance of the detailed specifications in the law, and a related failure to take context into account:

> *"Words having universal scope, such as 'every contract in restraint of trade,' 'every person who shall monopolize,' etc., will be taken, as a matter of course, to mean only everyone subject to such legislation, not all that the legislator subsequently may be able to catch."* United States Supreme Court, American Banana Co. v. United Fruit Co., 213 U.S. 347 (1909).

It is also supported by general ignorance as to the fact that the federal government is well and thoroughly stocked with workers in every imaginable "profession, trade, employment, or vocation" (all of whose federally-connected earnings are, of course, subject to the tax, and are, of course, those being considered in the relevant references). Visiting http://jobsearch.usajobs.opm.gov will quickly correct that misunderstanding... (Additional material related to this subject will be found below in the supplemental discussion of the definition of "trade or business".)

*****

A Note Regarding the Code Language About Refunds

No one should be misled by the fact that in certain sections of the IRC representation of the law only "taxpayers" are mentioned in regard to filing a claim for refund. Like much of the code, the relevant sections are compilations of several different statutes-in-force, a couple of which specify that they only apply to "taxpayers", and others of which do not. In the interests of brevity (or misdirection-- you decide), the code draftsmen wrote these sections so as to make them appear to apply only to "taxpayers". 26 USC 6511 is a good example. It (pertinently) reads as follows:

> *(a) Period of limitation on filing claim*
> *Claim for credit or refund of an overpayment of any tax imposed by this title in respect of which tax the taxpayer is required to file a return shall be filed by the taxpayer within 3 years from the time the return was filed or 2 years from the time the tax was paid, whichever of such periods expires the later, or if no return was filed by the taxpayer, within 2 years from the time the tax was paid. Claim for credit or refund of an overpayment of any tax imposed by this title which is required to be paid by means of a stamp shall be filed by the taxpayer within 3 years from the time the tax was paid.*

However, the refund statutes pertinent to most private-sector persons-- which are among those compiled in 26 USC

appearance in federal revenue law in reference to federally licensed activities, of which there were many in the early days of the "income" tax-- dozens and dozens, in fact. Today, the list of such activities is now confined to only a few, chiefly involving alcohol, tobacco and firearms.

Here is how some of the relevant statues were presented in the Revenue Act of 1873:

TITLE XXXV.—INTERNAL REVENUE.—CH. 3. 621

SEC. 3232. No person shall be engaged in or carry on any trade or business hereinafter mentioned until he has paid a special tax therefor in the manner hereinafter provided. Trade or business not to be carried on until tax paid.

13 July, 1866, c. 184, s. 9, v. 14, p. 113. 8 *May*, 1876, *J. R. No.* 10, *v.* 19, *p.* 213.—The License Tax Cases, 5 Wall., 462; U. S. *v.* Pressy, 1 Low., 319.

SEC. 3233. Every person engaged in any trade or business on which a special tax is imposed by law shall register with the collector of the district his name or style, place of residence, trade or business, and the place where such trade or business is to be carried on. In case of a firm or company, the names of the several persons constituting the same, and their places of residence, shall be so registered. Trade or business to be registered. 13 July, 1866, c. 184, s. 9, v. 14, p. 113. 24 Dec., 1872, c. 13, s. 1, v. 17, p. 401.

SEC. 3234. Any number of persons doing business in copartnership at any one place shall be required to pay but one special tax. Persons in partnership at same place liable for only one tax.

13 July, 1866, c. 184, s. 9, v. 14, p. 115.

SEC. 3235. The payment of the special tax imposed shall not exempt from an additional special tax the person carrying on a trade or business in any other place than that stated in the collector's register; but nothing herein contained shall require a special tax for the storage of goods, wares, or merchandise in other places than the place of business, nor, except as hereinafter provided, for the sale by manufacturers or producers of their own goods, wares, and merchandise, at the place of production or manufacture, and at their principal office or place of business, provided no goods, wares, or merchandise shall be kept except as samples at said office or place of business. Payment of one special tax not to cover several places of business. 13 July, 1866, c. 184, s. 9, v. 14, p. 113.

SEC. 3236. Whenever more than one of the pursuits or occupations hereinafter described are carried on in the same place by the same person at the same time, except as hereinafter provided, the tax shall be paid for each according to the rates severally prescribed. When more than one pursuit is carried on in same place by same person at same time.

13 July, 1866, c. 184, s. 9, v. 14, p. 114.

SEC. 3237. All special taxes shall become due on the first day of May, in each year, or on commencing any trade or business on which such tax is imposed. In the former case the tax shall be reckoned for one year; and in the latter case it shall be reckoned proportionately, from the first day of the month in which the liability to a special tax commenced to the first day of May following. When special tax to be due, how reckoned. 13 July, 1866, c. 184, s. 9, v. 14, p. 113. 6 June, 1872, c. 315, s. 31, v. 17, p. 252.

SEC. 3238. All special taxes imposed by law, including the tax on stills or worms, shall be paid by stamps denoting the tax, and the Commissioner of Internal Revenue is required to procure appropriate stamps for the payment of such taxes; and the provisions of sections thirty-three hundred and [*thirteen*] [twelve] and thirty-four hundred and forty-six, and all other provisions of law relating to the preparation and issue of stamps for distilled spirits, fermented liquors, tobacco, and cigars, shall, so far as applicable, extend to and include such stamps for special taxes; and the Commissioner of Internal Revenue shall have authority to make all needful regulations relative thereto. Stamps for special taxes. 20 July, 1868, c. 186, ss. 26, 101, v. 15, pp. 137, 165. 24 Dec., 1872, c. 13, s. 3, v. 17, p. 402. 18 *Feb.*, 1875, *c.* 80, *v.* 18, *p.* 319.

SEC. 3239. Every person engaged in any business, avocation, or employment, who is thereby made liable to a special tax, except tobacco peddlers, shall place and keep conspicuously in his establishment or place of business all stamps denoting the payment of said special tax; and any person who shall, through negligence, fail to so place and keep said [*stamp*] [stamps], shall be liable to a penalty equal to the special tax for which his business rendered him liable, and the costs of prosecution; but in no case shall said penalty be less than ten dollars. And where the failure to comply with the foregoing provision of law shall be through willful neglect or refusal, then the penalty shall be double the amount above prescribed: *Provided*, That nothing in this section shall in any way affect the liability of any person for exercising or carrying on any trade, business, or profession, or doing any act for the exercising, carrying on, or doing of which a special tax is imposed by law, without the payment thereof.	Special-tax stamp to be exhibited in place of business. 24 Dec., 1872, c. 13, s.3, v.17, p.402. 27 *Feb.*, 1877, c. 69, *v.* 19, *p.* 248.

(Note the use of "avocations", "employment", and "professions" as references to engaging in these special taxed activities, a usage which contributes to a further understanding of the context within which these terms are used elsewhere in the internal revenue laws.)

The code representation of the current version of these laws is compiled into Subtitle E. This is where the code-wide definition of "trade or business" as *"the performance of the functions of a public office"* might arguably be described as "manifestly incompatible with the intent thereof", and the meaning of the term for purposes of procedural requirements etc. be expanded to included those involved in the licensed activities. Those holding such licenses should keep this specialized distinction in mind.

That said, the phrase "trade or business" IS explicitly defined as solely "the performance of the functions of a public office" in the Revenue Act of 1938. It is this statute to which the relevant section of the IRC derivation tables exclusively points.

A Letter From The Social Security Administration

TEH2 [illegible] 23, 1998

Dear Mr.

This is in response to your letter concerning the requirement and use of the Social Security number (SSN).

The Social Security Act does not require a person to have a Social Security number (SSN) to live and work in the United States, nor does it require an SSN simply for the purpose of having one. However, if someone works without an SSN, we cannot properly credit the earnings for the work performed.

Other laws require people to have and use SSNs for specific purposes. For example, the Internal Revenue Code (26 U.S.C. 6109 (a)) and applicable regulations (26 CFR 301.6109-1(d)) require an individual to get and use an SSN on tax documents and to furnish the number to any other person or institution (such as an employer or a bank) that is required to provide the Internal Revenue Service (IRS) information about payments to the individual. There are penalties for failure to do so. The IRS also requires employers to report SSNs with employees' earnings.

The requirements for including the SSN as the taxpayer identification number on individual tax returns and on tax reports made by employers, banks, and other financial institutions are set by law or regulations of the Department of the Treasury. Anyone who has questions or objections to providing an SSN for these purposes should contact the nearest Internal Revenue Service office.

Sincerely,

Charles H. Mullen
Associate Commissioner
Office of Public Inquiries

A Lawful Direct Tax

STATUTE II.

CHAP. LXXV.—*An Act to lay and collect a direct tax within the United States.* July 14, 1798.

SECTION 1. *Be it enacted by the Senate and House of Representatives of the United States of America in Congress assembled,* That a direct tax of two millions of dollars shall be, and hereby is laid upon the United States, and apportioned to the states respectively, in the manner following:—

[Obsolete.] Act of July 9, 1798, ch. 70. A direct tax of two millions laid. 1802, ch. 12. Apportionment.

To the state of New Hampshire, seventy-seven thousand seven hundred and five dollars, thirty-six cents and two mills.

To the state of Massachusetts, two hundred and sixty thousand four hundred and thirty-five dollars, thirty-one cents and two mills.

To the state of Rhode Island, thirty-seven thousand five hundred and two dollars and eight cents.

To the state of Connecticut, one hundred and twenty-nine thousand seven hundred and sixty-seven dollars, and two mills.

To the state of Vermont, forty-six thousand eight hundred and sixty-four dollars eighteen cents and seven mills.

To the state of New York, one hundred and eighty-one thousand six hundred and eighty dollars, seventy cents and seven mills.

To the state of New Jersey, ninety-eight thousand three hundred and eighty-seven dollars, twenty-five cents, and three mills.

To the state of Pennsylvania, two hundred and thirty-seven thousand one hundred and seventy-seven dollars, seventy-two cents and seven mills.

To the state of Delaware, thirty thousand four hundred and thirty dollars, seventy-nine cents, and two mills.

To the state of Maryland, one hundred and fifty-two thousand five hundred and ninety-nine dollars, ninety-five cents, and four mills.

To the state of Virginia, three hundred and forty-five thousand four hundred and eighty-eight dollars, sixty-six cents, and five mills.

To the state of Kentucky, thirty-seven thousand six hundred and forty-three dollars, ninety-nine cents, and seven mills.

To the state of North Carolina, one hundred and ninety-three thousand six hundred and ninety-seven dollars, ninety-six cents, and five mills.

To the state of Tennessee, eighteen thousand eight hundred and six dollars, thirty-eight cents, and three mills.

To the state of South Carolina, one hundred and twelve thousand nine hundred and ninety-seven dollars, seventy-three cents and nine mills.

And to the state of Georgia, thirty-eight thousand eight hundred and fourteen dollars, eighty-seven cents, and five mills.

*****

A Brief Comment On Union-State "Income" Taxes

I have spent no time in this book on the "income" tax as it relates to the several States. However, all of the State law at which I have looked is fundamentally and explicitly dependent upon the initial application of the federal law in its operation. That is, the union-State taxation of "income" involves the adoption by the State of whatever amount of "income" has been arrived at by the citizen through application of the relevant federal law. A typical structure for this regime will require the citizen to transfer the "adjusted gross income" figure from the appropriate line on his or her previously completed federal 1040 to the "taxable income" line on the State return.

As a consequence, our examination herein of the federal law will, in many (if not all) cases, amount to a sufficient analysis of union-State "income" tax law as well. I leave to each individual reader any necessary supplemental investigation of a particular State law, confident that anyone who has made it to this point in this book will find the task simple enough.

Form 1099-MISC

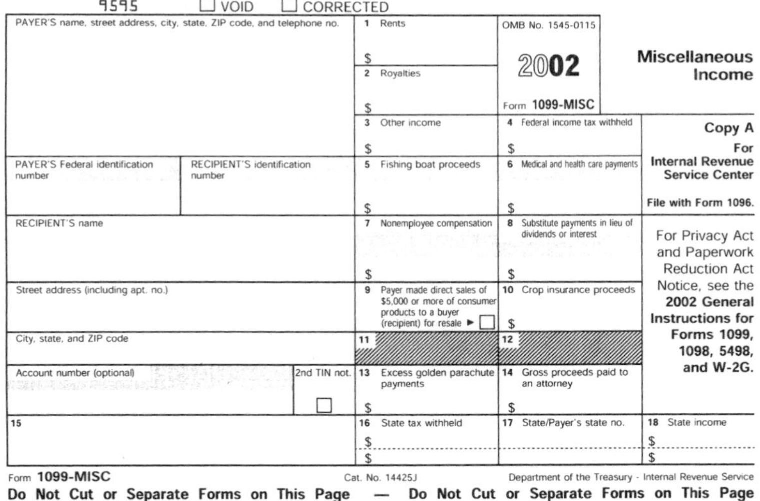

9595 ☐ VOID ☐ CORRECTED

PAYER'S name, street address, city, state, ZIP code, and telephone no.

1 Rents $

2 Royalties $

OMB No. 1545-0115

2002

Form 1099-MISC

Miscellaneous Income

3 Other income $

4 Federal income tax withheld $

Copy A For Internal Revenue Service Center

File with Form 1096.

PAYER'S Federal identification number

RECIPIENT'S identification number

5 Fishing boat proceeds $

6 Medical and health care payments $

RECIPIENT'S name

7 Nonemployee compensation $

8 Substitute payments in lieu of dividends or interest $

For Privacy Act and Paperwork Reduction Act Notice, see the **2002 General Instructions for Forms 1099, 1098, 5498, and W-2G.**

Street address (including apt. no.)

9 Payer made direct sales of $5,000 or more of consumer products to a buyer (recipient) for resale ► ☐

10 Crop insurance proceeds $

City, state, and ZIP code

11

12

Account number (optional)

2nd TIN not. ☐

13 Excess golden parachute payments $

14 Gross proceeds paid to an attorney $

15

16 State tax withheld $ $

17 State/Payer's state no.

18 State income $ $

Form 1099-MISC Cat. No. 14425J Department of the Treasury - Internal Revenue Service

Do Not Cut or Separate Forms on This Page — Do Not Cut or Separate Forms on This Page

Form 4852

Form **4852** (Revised Oct. 1998)	Department of the Treasury - Internal Revenue Service **Substitute for Form W-2, Wage and Tax Statement, or Form 1099-R, Distributions From Pensions, Annuities, Retirement or Profit-Sharing Plans, IRAs, Insurance Contracts, Etc.** **Attach to Form 1040,1040A, 1040-EZ or 1040X**	**OMB No. 1545-0458**

1. Name *(First, middle, last)* — 2. Social security number *(SSN)*

3. Address

4 **Please fill in the year at the end of the statement.** I have been unable to obtain (or have received an incorrect) Form W-2, Wage and Tax Statement, or Form 1099-R, Distributions From Pensions, Annuities, Retirement or Profit-sharing Plans IRA's, Insurance Contracts, etc., from my employer or payer named below. I have notified the Internal Revenue Service of this fact. The amounts shown below are my best estimates of all wages or payments paid to me and Federal taxes withheld by this employer or payer during________ *(year)*.

5. Employer's or payer's name, address and ZIP code — 6. Employer's or payer's identification number *(if known)*

7(A) Enter wages, compensations and taxes withheld

a. Wages (Note: Include (1) the total wages paid (2) noncash payments, (3) tips /reported and (4) all other compensation before deductions for taxes, insurance, etc.) ________

b. Social security wages ________

c. Medicare wages ________

d. Advance EIC payments ________

e. Social security tips ________

f. Federal income tax withheld ________

g. State tax withheld (Name or state) ________ ________

h. Local tax withheld (Name of locality) ________ ________

i. Social security tax withheld ________

j. Medicare tax withheld ________

7(B). Enter distributions from pensions, annuities, retirement or profit-sharing plans, IRAs, insurance contracts, etc.

1. Gross Distribution ________
2a Taxable Amount ________
2b. Taxable Amount not determined ☐
Total Distribution ☐
3. Capital Gains *(included in 2a)* ________
4. Federal Income Tax Withheld ________
5. State Income Tax Withheld ________
6. Employee Contribution ________
7. Net Unrealized Appreciation ________
8. Enter Distribution Code ________

8. How did you determine the amounts in item 7 above?

9. Explain your efforts to obtain Form W-2, 1099-R, or W-2c, Statement of Corrected Income and Tax Amounts.

Importance Notice: If your employer has ceased operations or filed for bankruptcy, you may wish to send a copy of this form to the Social Security Administration office listed in your telephone directory to ensure proper social security credit.

Paperwork Reduction Act Notice:
We ask for the information on this form to carry out the Internal Revenue laws of the United States. You are required to give us the information. We need it to ensure that you are complying with these laws and to allow us to figure and collect the right amount of tax. You are not required to provide the information requested on a form that is subject to the Paper Reduction Act unless the form displays a valid OMB control number. Books or records is relating to a form or its instructions must be retained as long as their contents may become material in the administration of any Internal Revenue law. Generally, tax returns and return information are confidential, as required by Code section 6103. The time needed to complete this form will vary depending on individual circumstances. The estimated average time is 18 minutes. If you have comments concerning the occurrence of this time estimate or suggestions for making this form simpler, we would be happy to hear from you. You can write to the Tax Forms Committee, Western Area Distribution Center, Rancho Cordova, CA 95743 0001. DO NOT send this form to this office. Instead, attach it to your tax return.

Under penalties of perjury, I declare that I have examined this statement, and to the best of my knowledge and belief, it is true, correct, and complete.

10. Your signature — 11. Date *(mmddyyyy)*

Catalog No. 42058U — Form **4852** (Rev. 10-98)

The United States Supreme Court On The Meaning Of 'Capitations'

The United States Supreme Court has explicitly declared the definition of 'capitations' as the term is used in Article 1, Section 9 of the United States Constitution:

> *"No Capitation, or other direct, Tax shall be laid, unless in Proportion to the Census or Enumeration herein before directed to be taken."*

Explaining the term in its exhaustive ruling on the federal taxing authority in Pollock v. Farmer's Loan & Trust, 157 U.S. 429 (1895), and citing the work of Albert Gallatin-- Pennsylvania state congressman, United States Representative and Senator, United States Minister to England and France, respectively, and the longest serving Secretary of the Treasury in American history-- as authoritative, the court observes that,

> *"...Albert Gallatin, in his Sketch of the Finances of the United States, published in November, 1796, said: 'The most generally received opinion, however, is that, by direct taxes in the constitution, those are meant which are raised on the capital or revenue of the people;...'*
>
> *...*
>
> *"He then quotes from Smith's Wealth of Nations, and continues: 'The remarkable coincidence of the clause of the constitution with this passage in using the word 'capitation' as a generic expression, including the different species of direct taxes-- an acceptation of the word peculiar, it is believed, to Dr. Smith-- leaves little doubt that the framers of the one had the other in view at the time, and that they, as well as he, by direct taxes, meant those paid directly from the falling immediately on the revenue;...'"*

Additional Material

In order to keep this book as affordable as possible (as well as to provide for the addition of supplemental material as it becomes available), the many highly important additional pages of appendix materials and resources associated with '**Cracking the Code-...**' will be found on the web at **www.losthorizons.com**

Posted topics include:

- The wonderful successes in upholding the law enjoyed by readers across America since this book first went to print;
- Government efforts to discourage those readers, and to suppress this book;
- Discussions of various 'tax protestor' misunderstandings;
- The current form of section 93 of the 1862 revenue act;
- Further discussions of W-4s; the application and mechanics of the levy, summons, and examination/audit powers; and other subjects dealt with in 'Cracking the Code-...'
- Frequently asked questions;

...and much, much more.

My Best Wishes Are With You All